FOOTBALL ENGLISH
ELEMENTARY

SELF-STUDY WORKBOOK

Peter Clements

SUPPORTED BY:

Copyright ©2022 HATRIQA Limited

All rights reserved. Apart from any use permitted under UK copyright law, no part of this publication may be reproduced, stored in a retrieval system, or transmitted in any form or by any means, electronic or mechanical, including photocopying, recording, or otherwise without prior written permission from the Publisher or under license permitting restricted copying in the United Kingdom from the Copyright Licensing Agency Limited. Further details of such licenses (for reprographic reproduction) may be obtained from the Copyright Licensing Agency Limited, www.cla.co.uk.

ISBN 9781915791009

Published by HATRIQA Limited
Lower Ground Floor
7 Coleherne Road
London SW10 9BS

PUBLISHER Tim Gentles
ILLUSTRATIONS Marcus Marritt
DESIGN AND TYPESETTING Lucy Allen

Special thanks to Hank Steinbrecher, Joan Laporta, Emma Jones MBE, The Enterprise Nation Bus, Felipe Anderson, Dan Freedman, Alison Edgar MBE, Issei Yokoi, Andy Downer, UCL Institute of Education, UCL EDUCATE, UCL Innovation and Enterprise

Orders are available through our website at www.hatriqa.com or by emailing orders@hatriqa.com.

A catalogue record for this title is available from the British Library.

Contents

	How to Learn Vocabulary	5
	Core Football Vocabulary	6
UNIT 1	**Player Positions and Personal Information**	10
UNIT 2	**Football Actions**	15
UNIT 3	**Rules of the Game**	20
UNIT 4	**Football Kit**	25
UNIT 5	**Daily Routine**	30
Review	Units 1–5	35
UNIT 6	**The Body**	38
UNIT 7	**Describing Players**	43
UNIT 8	**Playing in a Game**	48
UNIT 9	**After the Game**	53
UNIT 10	**Fixtures and Results**	58
Review	Units 6–10	63
	Grammar Reference	66
	Irregular Verbs	78
	Wordlists	79
	Answer Key	86

How to Learn Vocabulary

A. Write down words that go together (collocations)

You **play football**. Sometimes, you may **shoot the ball** and **score a goal**.

When words are used together like this, we call it a **collocation**.

- You play **in midfield**, but play **at the back** (= defence).
  – preposition + noun
- Some players are **good at** free kicks (NOT ~~good in~~).
  – adjective + preposition
- Van der Sar was a very **tall goalkeeper** (NOT ~~high goalkeeper~~).
  – adjective + noun

Tip: Always write down collocations when you learn a new word.

B. Learn words in families

Word family	Words in family
pitch	goal, centre circle, halfway line, penalty area
kit	boots, shirt, shorts, socks, shin pads

C. Draw pictures and diagrams

Draw pictures. For example: 4–4–2

```
X X X X
X X X X
 X X
```

Draw diagrams like this one.

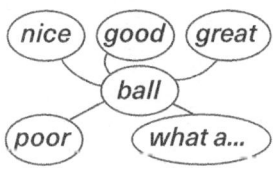

Add more words as you learn them.

Core Football Vocabulary

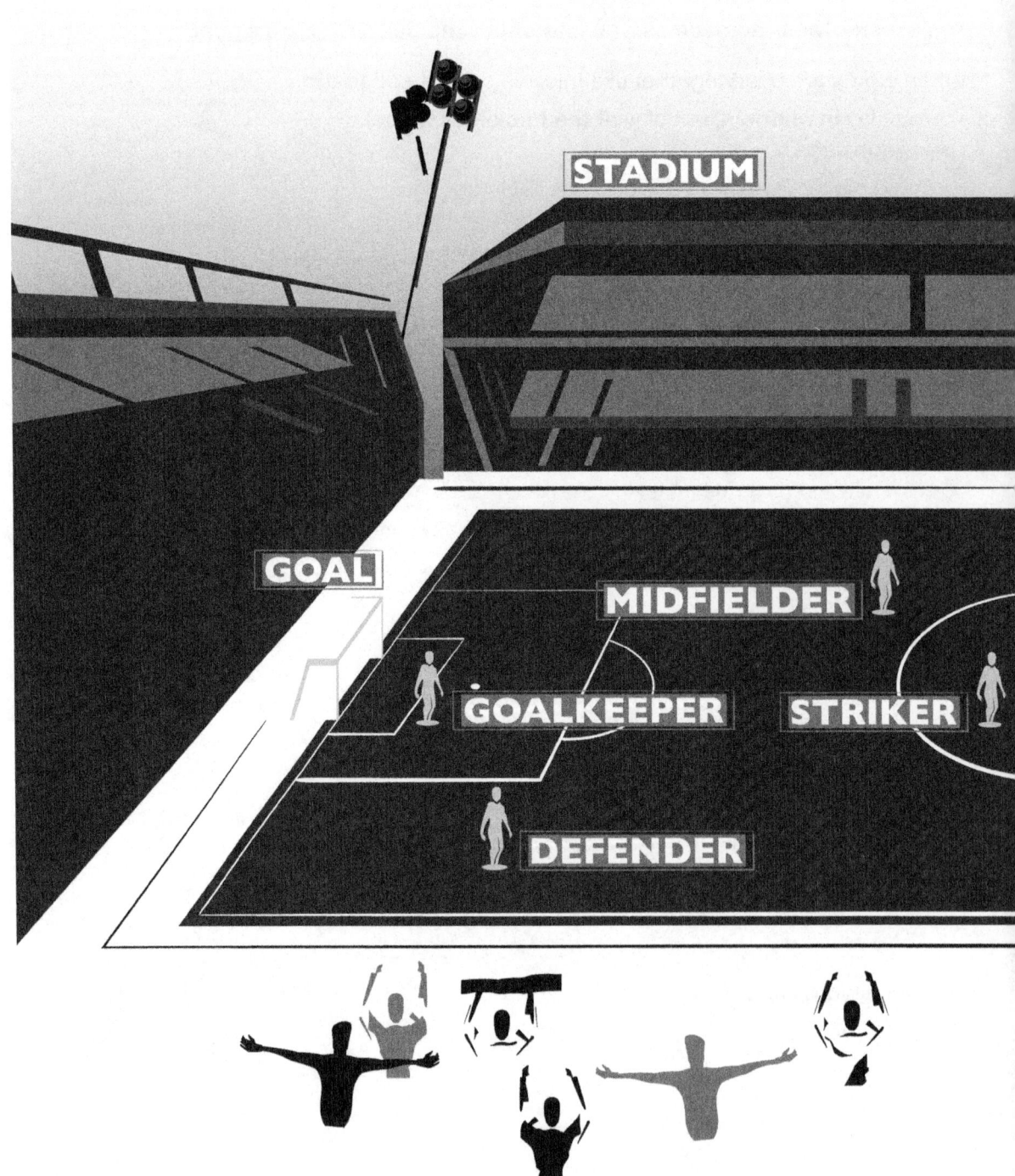

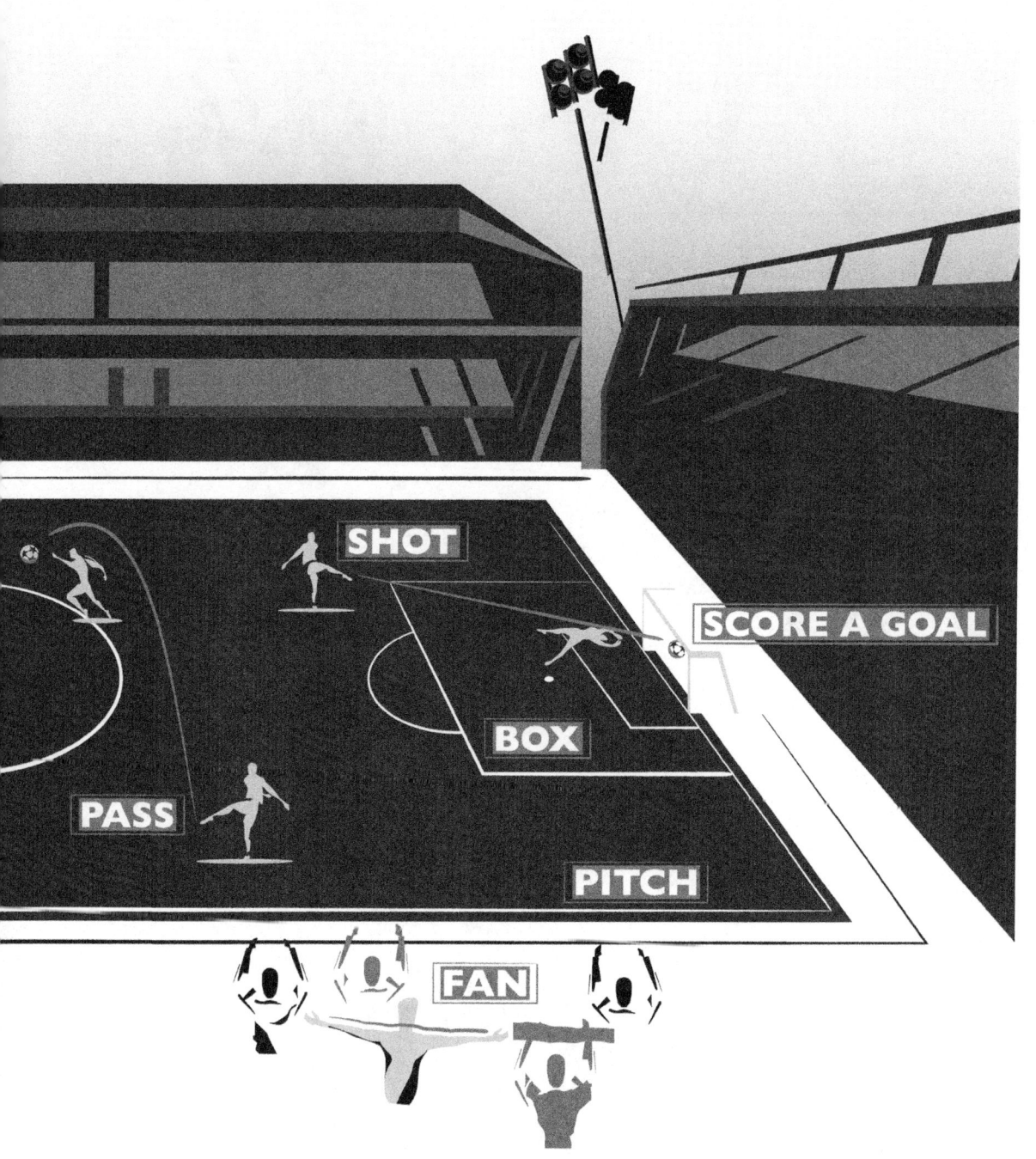

Core Football Vocabulary

Core Football Vocabulary

UNIT 1

Player Positions and Personal Information

Vocabulary

Exercise 1

Read the text. Complete each player's number.

	Number		Number
Sarah	_1_	Haruka	___
Hannah	___	Rachel	___
Marta	___	Meghan	___
Lucy	___ (c)	Mia	___
Kim	___	Yuna	___
Emma	___		

Here are the players and positions for the Locomotive London game today. The **goalkeeper**, as always, is Sarah. The **left full back** is Hannah, and **on the right of defence** is Marta. The **centre backs** are Kim and Lucy. Lucy wears the number 5 shirt and is the **team captain**. In **central midfield** Locomotive have Emma wearing number 6, and Haruka next to her as an **attacking central midfielder**. The **left winger** is Rachel, with Meghan in **right midfield**. Star **striker** and number 9, Mia, is with Yuna up front.

Exercise 2

Complete the sentences about players in your team.

Examples:

The goalkeeper is Sarah.
The centre backs are Kim and Lucy.
Haruka wears the number 8 shirt.

The goalkeeper is _____. The centre backs are _____ and _____.
_____ wears the number _____ shirt.

Your idea: _____

UNIT 1 | Player Positions and Personal Information

Vocabulary Building

Exercise 1

Rearrange these words to make questions about personal information.

1. phone / number / What's / your ? **Question:** _____
2. What's / email / address / your ? **Question:** _____
3. use / you / Do / WhatsApp ? **Question:** _____
4. on / Instagram / you / Are ? **Question:** _____
5. I / Can / you / add / Facebook / on ? **Question:** _____
6. Do / follow / you / on / Marcus Rashford / Twitter ?
   Question: _____

Exercise 2

a. Complete the information for rows **1–4** in the table. Then add two more countries and complete the information for **5–6**.

	Country	Nationality	Example player
1.	Argentina		
2.	Portugal		
3.		South Korean	
4.	Italy		
5.			
6.			

b. Choose the correct options to complete the sentences.

1. Cristiano Ronaldo is *Portuguese / Portugal*. He's from *Portuguese / Portugal*.
2. Mia Hamm is from *the USA / American*. She's *the USA / American*.
3. Riyad Mahrez is *Algeria / Algerian*. He's from *Algerian / Algeria*.
4. Alexia Putellas is from *Spain / Spanish*. She's *Spain / Spanish*.

Grammar

Exercise 1

Choose the correct words to complete the football facts.

1. Lionel Messi *is / are / isn't* from Argentina.
2. Harry Kane *is / isn't / aren't* a midfielder.
3. David De Gea *is / isn't / are* a goalkeeper.
4. Eden and Thorgan Hazard *is / are / aren't* from Belgium.
5. Arsenal *is / are / aren't* a team in the English Premier League.
6. Pro Evolution Soccer *are / is / not* a popular football video game.
7. VAR *is / are / aren't* used in the Bundesliga.

> **Don't forget!**
> When we say "VAR" (Video Assistant Referee) we say each letter. It sounds like "VEE-AY-AR".

Exercise 2

Read the conversation between a referee on the pitch and a video assistant referee (VAR). Complete the conversation with the correct form of the verb *be*.

Referee: 1. ___*Is*___ Miguel offside?

VAR: We 2. _____ watching the replay now.

Referee: OK.

VAR: Please wait...

VAR: OK. When Harry passes the ball, Miguel 3. _____ offside. He's level with the defender. The goal is good. Give the goal.

Referee: 4. _____ you sure?

VAR: Yes, we 5. _____ sure. Miguel 6. _____ onside. I repeat, onside. It 7. _____ a goal.

Referee: OK. Thanks.

> **Did you know?**
> *Match officials* is the general term for the referee and their assistants.

Exercise 3

Here are the answers – what are the questions?

Question	Answer
1. _____?	My name is Miguel.
2. _____?	I'm from Spain.
3. _____?	I'm 29.
4. _____?	I'm a defender. I can play at centre back or left back.
5. _____?	My favourite player is Lionel Messi. He's amazing!

UNIT 1 | Player Positions and Personal Information

Reading

Exercise 1

Read the transfer news about Locomotive London.
Do they want to buy a defender? *Yes / No*

SPORT
Home | Football | Cricket | Tennis | Athletics

Locomotive London Transfer News

Locomotive London want to sign 35-year-old Brazilian international Roberto. The left-footed midfielder can play in central midfield or as a winger. He has 40 caps for Brazil and 15 goals.
(Source: The Daily Rabona)

Locomotive want to sign star striker Kim Hee Deok in January. Kim, 21, is from South Korea and plays for Korean League club, Busan Spartans. This season he has 17 goals in 15 games, including five goals in the Asian Champions League. *(Source: Nutmegs Weekly)*

Harry and Jack aren't happy at Locomotive London. Jack is a centre back, but the manager wants him to play in a different position. Harry is unhappy because he isn't playing every game. Sporting Madrid are interested in both players. *(Source: The Sunday Sub)*

Locomotive London want to buy Belgian brothers Alex and Vincent Danger. Alex is an attacking central midfielder, and Vincent is a winger. Liège Royals player Alex is the captain of the national team and will cost over 80 million euros. Vincent is available for free after leaving Sporting Madrid.
(Source: Locomotive London Fanzine)

Exercise 2

Read the transfer news again. (Circle) the correct answers.

1. Which two footballers play for their national team?
   Roberto   Kim Hee Deok   Alex Danger
2. Which two players are wingers?
   Roberto   Vincent   Jack
3. Which two footballers do Sporting Madrid want to buy?
   Harry   Jack   Vincent Danger
4. Which player costs nothing?
   Alex Danger   Vincent Danger   Kim Hee Deok
5. Which player wants to play more football?
   Roberto   Vincent Danger   Harry

UNIT 1 | Player Positions and Personal Information

Exercise 3

a. Which of the players in the transfer news sound good? Why?

I think _____ sounds good, because _____

b. Which player in world football do you want your club to buy? Why?

I want my club to buy _____, because _____

My Learning

New Words

New word from Unit 1	Translation

Quick Quiz

- Think of 3 types of midfielder: _____
- List 4 countries and their nationalities: _____
  _____
- What does a video assistant referee do? Explain their job in your first language.
  _____

Reflection

I can understand language to describe positions on the football pitch. ☹ 😐 ☺
I can use the correct form of the verb *be* to talk about footballers and teams. ☹ 😐 ☺
I can understand a short text about transfer news. ☹ 😐 ☺

In Unit 1, I enjoyed *talking about player positions / learning to use* be *in the present simple / talking about personal information / other:* [   ]

I want to know more about *player positions / sharing personal information / talking about transfers / other:* [   ]

Choose 2 ways to practise Unit 1:

☐ I'll ask people about their positions on the pitch.

☐ I'll write 5 sentences about my favourite players, their nationalities and their positions.

☐ I'll read the transfer news about my club in English.

☐ My idea: [   ]

UNIT 2

Football Actions

Vocabulary

Exercise 1

Complete the diagram with the words from the box.

mark   clear
pass   shoot
head   save
cross tackle

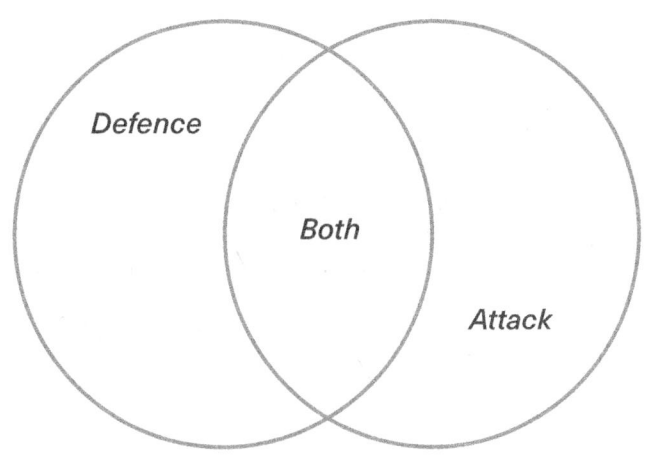

Exercise 2

a. Draw a picture for sentences **1–3**.

Example: Harry passes to Jack.	1. Lucy tackles Meghan.	2. Miguel shoots and the goalkeeper saves!
3. Luca crosses from the left.	4. _____	5. _____

b. Write your own sentences for **4–5**, then draw pictures for the sentences. Use the words from the box for ideas.

clear   mark   foul   cross   head   dribble

UNIT 2 | Football Actions

Vocabulary Building

Exercise 1

a. Complete the table with the noun form for each verb. Use a dictionary to help you.

Verb	Noun
save	*save*
tackle	*tackle*
pass	
cross	
shoot	
head	
clear	

> **Did you know?**
> We often use these words to describe a goalkeeper's actions: *save*, *catch*, *punch*. How do you say these words in your first language?

b. Choose the best noun from the table to complete each sentence.

1. Miguel has the ball. He's outside the penalty box. He has a _____. Oh! What a wonderful goal!
2. The cross comes in. Jack jumps high! He scores with a _____. Oh no, off the post!
3. The goalkeeper punches high and far. That's a good _____.
4. The winger dribbles past the full back. It's a great _cross_ into the box for the forward... and he scores! One–nil to Locomotive!
5. The forward runs into the box, but across comes the defender. Oh, what a _____ by the Locomotive centre back! Fantastic defending! And the score stays at nil–nil.

Grammar

Exercise 1

a. Sergio and Riccardo are talking about their teammate, Juan. Complete the conversation with the correct form of each verb.

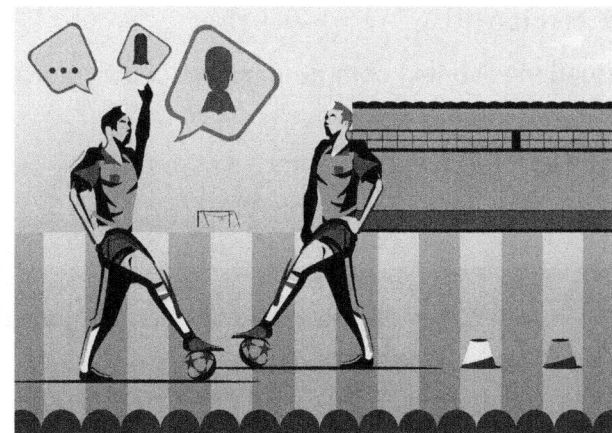

Sergio: Juan always [1.] _shoots_ (shoot). He [2.] _____ (not / pass).

Riccardo: Really? He [3.] _____ (pass) to me. Anyway, what about you?! You never pass.

Sergio: Ha! I do!

Riccardo: You don't! When you get near the box you always [4.] _____ (shoot).

Sergio: I'm a team player Riccardo, you know that!

Riccardo: Haha, yeah sure! Juan is a team player. He helps the defence. He [5.] _____ (tackle). He [6.] _____ (mark) attackers when it's a corner. I [7.] _____ (not / see) you defending during matches...

Sergio: OK, that is true! Still, I do lots for the team. [8.] _____ (Do) Juan cross?

Riccardo: Well, no. But Juan plays in the centre. You [9.] _____ (be) a winger, so you [10.] _____ (cross) the ball more.

Sergio: I [11.] _____ (take) the free kicks.

Riccardo: We don't score from free kicks. Juan [12.] _____ (take) the corners. We score from corners.

Sergio: Oh! So you're saying Juan is better!

Riccardo: I'm not saying that...

b. Choose the correct options to complete the summary.

Riccardo jokes that Sergio [1.] *is / isn't* a team player. Sergio says Juan [2.] *is / isn't* a team player and that he always [3.] *shoot / shoots*. Sergio is a winger, so he often [4.] *cross / crosses* the ball. Riccardo says that Juan often [5.] *help / helps* the defence.

UNIT 2 | Football Actions

Reading

Exercise 1

Read the live-text commentary from Locomotive London v Manchester Athletic. Answer the questions.

1. What's the score after 18 minutes? _____
2. Who gets a red card? Why? _____

Live text | Locomotive London v Manchester Athletic

9 minutes: YELLOW CARD – LUCA
Luca tackles Brown on the halfway line. He misses the ball and kicks Brown's leg. That's an early yellow card for Luca. He needs to be careful now.

11 minutes: CHANCE!
Taka crosses the ball from the right. Harry controls the ball on his chest. He's near the penalty spot. He shoots. Ederson saves. Locomotive London look good!

13 minutes: GOAL! Locomotive London 0 – 1 Manchester Athletic
Terrible defending! Farlen passes to Silamino on the left. Silamino crosses. Nobody marks Michael in the centre. Michael heads into the net. Athletic lead.

17 minutes: CHANCE!
Miguel takes a corner from the right. Jack heads at goal. Silamino clears off the goal line!

18 minutes: VAR CHECK!
Wait! There's a VAR check. Did Silamino use his hand to clear the ball?

18 minutes: PENALTY TO LOCOMOTIVE! RED CARD SILAMINO!
Silamino is sent off! Miguel has a chance to make it 1–1.

Exercise 2

Read the text again. Are the sentences true (T) or false (F)?

1. Luca gets a yellow card for a tackle on Silamino. T/F
2. Harry shoots from inside the box. T/F
3. Michael scores with his left foot. T/F
4. Jack takes corners for Locomotive London. T/F
5. Silamino uses his hand to stop Harry's header. T/F

> **Did you know?**
> When someone gets a *red card*, we say *they're sent off*. For a *yellow card*, we say *they're booked*.

UNIT 2 | Football Actions

Exercise 3

What happens next? Write the next live-text update.

19 minutes: _____

My Learning

New Words

New word from Unit 2	Translation

Quick Quiz

- List 5 actions footballers do: _____
- Complete the verb pattern: *I tackle; You tackle; He/She* _____.
- Name 3 players who tackle a lot: _____

Reflection

I can understand language to describe football actions.	☹ 😐 🙂
I can use the correct form of present simple verbs to talk about football actions.	☹ 😐 🙂
I can understand a live-text commentary about a football match.	☹ 😐 🙂

In Unit 2, I enjoyed _____

I want to know more about _____

Choose 2 ways to practise Unit 2:

- ☐ I'll ask people about their actions on the pitch.
- ☐ I'll write 5 sentences about my / my favourite player's actions on the pitch.
- ☐ I'll read the live-text commentary updates from my team's next match in English.
- ☐ My idea: _____

UNIT 3

Rules of the Game

Vocabulary

Exercise 1

Complete the table with the words from the box.

> throw-in   halfway line   touchline   kick-off
> centre circle   free kick   penalty   corner
> goal kick   penalty box

Set piece	Place on a football pitch
throw in, free kick, goal kick, corner, kick off, penalty	centre circle, penalty box, halfway line, touchline

Exercise 2

a. Match the situations (**1–5**) to the decisions (**a–e**).

Situation	Decision
1. The ball hits a defender and goes behind the goal.	a. It's a goal kick.
2. She shoots, but the ball goes over the goal.	b. It's a free kick.
3. He heads the ball over the touchline.	c. It's a corner.
4. Handball in the box!	d. It's a penalty.
5. That's a foul outside the box.	e. It's a throw-in.

2, 5, 1, 4, 3

b. Complete each line from the commentator with a decision from Exercise 2a.

1. Jack jumps for a header on the halfway line. The ball hits his arm.
   <u>It's a free kick.</u>

2. Miguel has an open goal. He shoots! Oh, he misses!
   <u>It's a goal kick</u>

3. Jack heads the ball over his own goal. <u>It's a own goal</u>

4. Harry pulls the striker's shirt in the box. The referee sees it. <u>It's a penalty</u>

5. The ball goes off the pitch near the halfway line.
   <u>It's a throw in</u>

UNIT 3 | Rules of the Game

Vocabulary Building

Exercise 1

a. Label the pictures with the words from the box.

crossbar
post
byline
penalty spot

 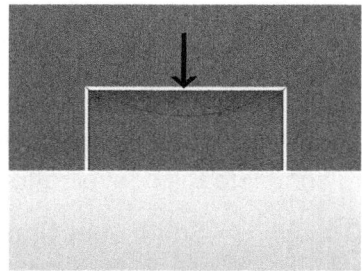

1. _____ 2. _____

b. You're the referee! What do you do? Complete the table below with the words from the box. You can choose more than one option or use your own ideas.

 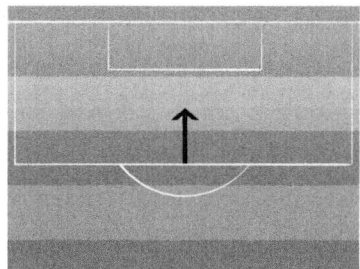

3. _____ 4. _____

free kick   penalty   yellow card
red card   goal kick   corner

Foul	Your decision
1. A player handballs in the centre circle.	*Free kick, no yellow card*
2. A defender pulls a striker's shirt in the box.	Penalty, red card
3. A player says a bad word to the referee.	sent off, red card
4. A defender uses their hand to push the ball over the **crossbar**.	Penalty, red card
5. A defender heads the ball against their own **post**! The ball goes over the **byline**.	own goal, no card
6. It's a penalty. The ball is on the **penalty spot**. An angry defender kicks the ball into the crowd!	sent off, red card

21

UNIT 3 | Rules of the Game

Grammar

Exercise 1

England are in a penalty shootout! The coach and his assistant are choosing the penalty takers. Choose the correct words to complete the conversation.

Coach: Smith goes first. He [1] *take / takes* the penalties for Liverpool City.

Assistant: Yes. Then Martin and Roberts. They sometimes [2] *take / takes* penalties for their club teams.

Coach: OK. So, who's number 4?

Assistant: Gordon?

Coach: Gordon doesn't [3] *take / takes* penalties for Newcastle Town.

Assistant: But he [4] *take / takes* good penalties in training.

Coach: OK, so Gordon is number 4. We've got Smith, Martin, Roberts, Gordon...

Assistant: Who [5] *take / takes* penalties for their club?

Coach: Um... Price [6] *take / takes* some penalties for Locomotive London.

Assistant: [7] *Do / Does* he score?

Coach: Yes. Price never [8] *miss / misses* penalties.

Assistant: OK, Price is number 5.

Don't forget!
When a verb ends in -*ch*, -*ss*, -*sh*, -*x* or -*zz*, we add -*es*: cross**es**, miss**es**, finish**es**.

Exercise 2

Answer the questions about set pieces in the box. Use full sentences.

1. Do you take penalties for your team?
   _____

2. Are you a good penalty taker?
   _____

3. Do you take any other set pieces?
   _____

4. Who is the best penalty taker you know? What makes them so good?
   _____

UNIT 3 | Rules of the Game

Reading

Exercise 1

Read the preview of Locomotive London's next game from newspaper *The Daily Goalpost*. Complete the summary.

> Jack Pearce thinks Newcastle Town will ¹·_____ the match. He says that Locomotive London will miss Miguel because he takes all of the ²·_____ for the team.

········· THE DAILY GOALPOST • Saturday 13th February ···

PREVIEW: LOCOMOTIVE LONDON v NEWCASTLE TOWN (3PM)

Locomotive London will miss Miguel

Jack Pearce, ex-Locomotive London and Newcastle Town striker, shares his views on today's match.

■ Set pieces are important in this game. Both teams score a lot of goals from set pieces. On average, Newcastle Town score one goal per game from free kicks or corners. They also score from long throw-ins. Locomotive London centre backs Luca and Jack mark well from free kicks, but it isn't easy to mark from long throw-ins.

Miguel's injury is a problem for Locomotive London. He's the best set-piece taker in the league at the moment. Miguel takes all Locomotive London's free kicks, corners and penalties. Miguel has 6 goals from penalties this season.

When Miguel doesn't play, Jack and Harry take free kicks and corners. It's better to have Jack and Harry in the box for set pieces. Both players often score from headers. Newcastle Town defend well from open play. Without Miguel's set pieces, I think it will be difficult for Locomotive London to score.

Prediction: Newcastle Town to win 2–0

Exercise 2

Read the text again. Draw a line through the wrong information in each sentence. Write the correct information in the space.

Example:

The match starts at ~~4pm~~. *3pm*

1. Locomotive London are the away team. _____
2. Newcastle Town score goals from goal kicks, corners and long throw-ins. _____
3. Locomotive London's central midfielders defend free kicks well. _____
4. Miguel has scored 6 free kicks this season. _____
5. Jack and Harry take set pieces when Miguel plays. _____
6. Jack and Harry never score from headers. _____

23

UNIT 3 | Rules of the Game

Exercise 3

How many words connected to set pieces can you find in the text? Add them to the box below.

free kick,

My Learning

New Words

New word from Unit 3	Translation

Quick Quiz

- List 5 set pieces: _____
- How many penalty takers can you name for club and/or country?
  _____
- How do you explain the offside rule in your first language? Can you explain it in English? _____
  _____

Reflection

I can understand language to describe the rules of the game.

I can use the correct form of present simple verbs to talk about the rules of the game.

I can understand the main ideas in a match preview.

In Unit 3, I enjoyed _____

I want to know more about _____

Choose 2 ways to practise Unit 3:

- ☐ I'll listen to commentary in English and write down words I hear from this unit.
- ☐ I'll write 5 sentences about the rules of the game.
- ☐ I'll read a preview for my team's next match in English.
- ☐ My idea: _____

UNIT 4
Football Kit

Vocabulary

Exercise 1

Label the goalkeeper's kit with the words from the box.

shorts   boots
socks   shirt
headband gloves

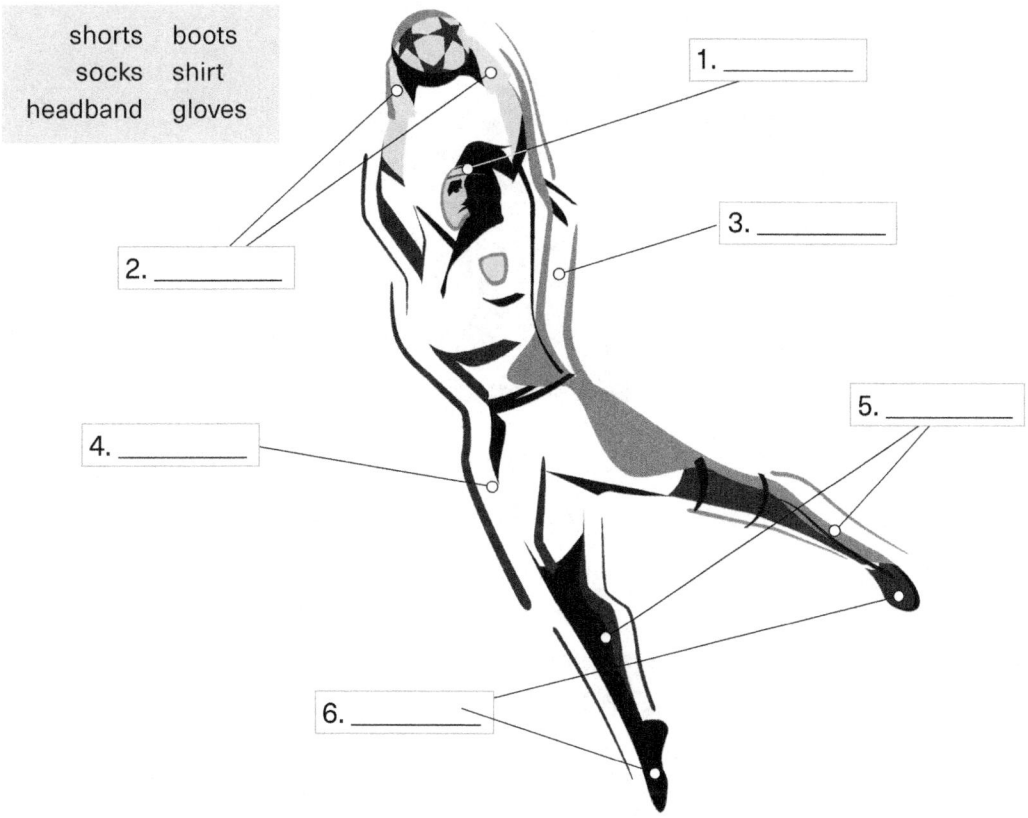

Exercise 2

Rearrange the letters to complete the information.

1. Manchester United play their home games in _red_____ (edr).
2. Bayern Munich play their home games in _____ (ulbe) and _____ (der).
3. Celtic play their home games in _____ (ergen) and _____ (hiwet).
4. AC Milan play their home games in _____ (dre) and _____ (lacbk).
5. Brazil's home kit is _____ (ellywo).
6. The Netherlands play their home matches in _____ (raeogn).

UNIT 4 | Football Kit

Vocabulary Building

Exercise 1

Label the shirt with the words from the box.

sleeves
badge
stripes
collar

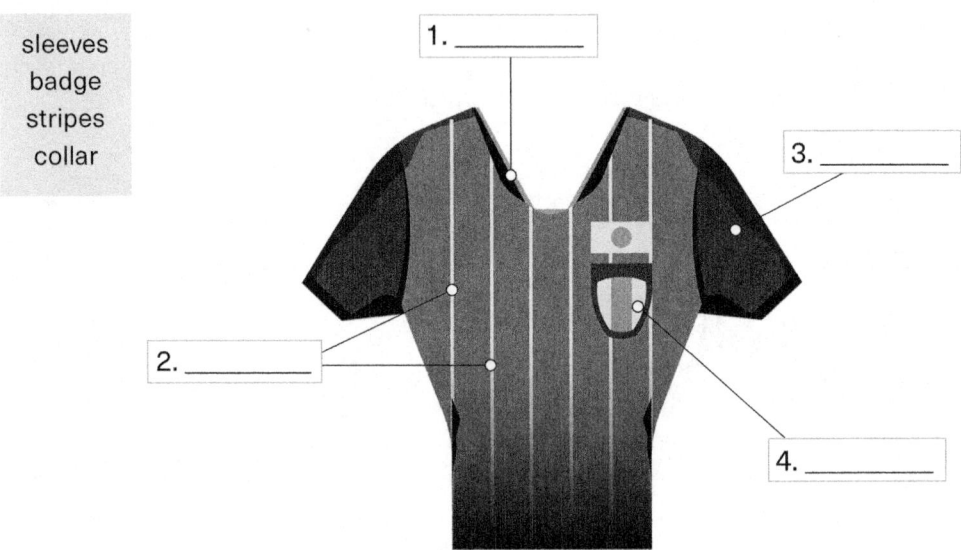

Exercise 2

How much do you know about team kits? Take this quick quiz.

1. Can you name a Serie A team that play in black and white **stripes**? _____
2. Can you name a team in La Liga whose home kit is all white? _____
3. True or false? Barcelona have **stripes** on their home shirt. _____
4. Which colour are the **sleeves** on Arsenal's home shirt? _____
5. Which top Bundesliga team play in yellow and black? _____
6. Which two World Cup-winning teams have birds on their **badge**? _____, _____

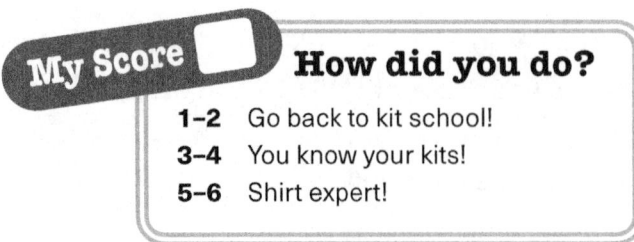

My Score ☐ **How did you do?**
- **1–2** Go back to kit school!
- **3–4** You know your kits!
- **5–6** Shirt expert!

UNIT 4 | Football Kit

Reading

Exercise 1

Read about Lisa Staley's activities on matchdays. How does Lisa help the players?

1. Lisa works as a _____.
2. Lisa makes sure that the _____ is ready for matchdays.

Lisa Staley — Locomotive London Kit Manager

Matchday Experiences

I ARRIVE at Champion Ground at around 11am on matchdays. First, I have an early lunch at the staff café. Then, I go to the laundry room to collect the team kits. We wash the kit on Fridays so it's ready for matchdays. Dave, my assistant, helps me bring the kit bags to the dressing room. We put the matchday kit for each player in their locker, then hang their shirts on the locker doors.

You might think this is an easy job, but it's not!

Luca asks us to put two pairs of socks in his locker. He wears one pair for the warm-up and another for the match! Harry always wants us to hang his Number 4 shirt last on the locker door. Jack's sock tape is always the same colour as the matchday shirt, and Liam gets angry if we forget his headband! Players these days…

Exercise 2

Read the text. Are these statements true (T) or false (F)?

1. After Lisa arrives at the stadium, she gets something to eat.
2. Lisa works alone.
3. Lisa puts the players' shirts in their lockers.
4. Luca changes some of his kit after the warm-up.
5. Jack wears yellow sock tape for home matches.

Exercise 3

Lisa said: "You might think this is an easy job, but it's not!" Why did she say this? Complete the sentence.

Lisa's job isn't easy because _____.

Grammar

Exercise 1

Liam and Jack are talking to Lisa, the Kit Manager. Choose the correct options to complete the conversation.

Liam: Lisa! Lisa!

Lisa: Yes, Liam?

Liam: 1. *Who / Whose* are these socks?

Lisa: Erm... I don't know. Are they 2. *you / yours*?

Liam: No! They aren't 3. *mine / my*! But they're in my locker!

Lisa: OK. Well, sorry about that. It's 4. *my / mine* mistake.

Jack: Those are Harry's socks.

Liam: Why are 5. *her / his* socks in my locker?

Jack: I don't know. Who cares? It's just some socks.

Liam: Lisa?

Lisa: ... Yes, Liam?

Liam: Where's my headband?

Lisa: That's it, there. Next to 6. *you / your* shirt.

Liam: That's not 7. *my / mine*! It's the wrong one! We are playing Liverpool City today.

Lisa: So?

Liam: 8. *This / Those* hairband is red. You know Liverpool City! 9. *Their / They* shirts are red! I can't wear a red hairband against Liverpool City. It's unlucky.

Lisa: OK, OK. I'll find you another hairband. Calm down, Liam!

Liam: Sorry. It's just... It's a big game today. I'm nervous.

Lisa: Oh wait, look! Is that hairband 10. *you / yours*? The one next to Jack's shirt.

Liam: That's it! Thanks Lisa.

Exercise 2

Rewrite the sentences to include possessive pronouns.

Example:

These are my boots. → *These boots are mine.*

1. That is your red shirt. → That red shirt is _____.
2. Those are your purple shin pads. → Those _____ are _____.
3. That's her black armband. → That _____.

4. Are these his socks? → Are _____?
5. These are our shirts. → _____
6. These are her gloves. → _____
7. Who do these socks belong to? → _____ are these socks?
8. These are their boots. → _____

My Learning

New Words

New word from Unit 4	Translation

Quick Quiz

- Name 8 items of football kit: _____
- Can you describe Brazil's home shirt? _____
- Which other items of football kit do you know in your first language? Do you know the words for this kit in English? _____

Reflection

I can understand language to describe football kits.	☹	😐	☺
I can use possessives to describe players' and teams' kits.	☹	😐	☺
I can understand a text about jobs in football.	☹	😐	☺

In Unit 4, I enjoyed [_____]

I want to know more about [_____]

Choose 2 ways to practise Unit 4:
- ☐ I'll design and label a new kit for my favourite team.
- ☐ I'll write 5 sentences about my favourite team's kit.
- ☐ I'll read about the Kit Manager at my favourite club.
- ☐ My idea: [_____]

UNIT 5

Daily Routine

Vocabulary

Exercise 1

a. Put the words below into the correct column.

~~breakfast~~ social media to bed football scores home
training a match to the gym free time shopping

have	check	go
breakfast		

b. Add two of your own ideas to each column. Use a dictionary to help you.

Exercise 2

a. Match the sentence parts in Column A with parts from Column B. Choose the best option. Write each complete sentence below.

Column A
1. I check social media
2. I usually go to bed
3. I go to the gym
4. My team usually have a match at

Column B
after work to keep fit!
about a hundred times a day!
3pm on Saturdays.
before 11pm.

1. _____
2. _____
3. _____
4. _____

b. Tick (✓) the sentences above that are true for you.

c. Write your own sentences about daily activities with phrases from Unit 5.
→ **Unit 5** Wordlist p81

1. _____
2. _____

UNIT 5 | Daily Routine

Vocabulary Building

Exercise 1

Each group of words in the table links to a daily activity from Unit 5. Which one? Translate any words you don't know.

have a match ~~have breakfast~~ go shopping
check social media have free time

Connected words	Activity
cereal, morning, toast	*have breakfast*
relax, play games, listen to music	
first half, half-time, second half	
buy clothes, pay, discount	
share, like, follow	

Grammar

Read the conversation between Miguel's agent and an editor from *London Today* newspaper. Complete the gaps with the present simple form of the verbs in brackets.

UNIT 5 | Daily Routine

Editor: We would like to interview Miguel about his move to Locomotive London.
Agent: Sure, Miguel is happy to talk with the media.
Editor: Can we speak with Miguel tomorrow morning?
Agent: What time?
Editor: At 9 o'clock?
Agent: I'm sorry. Miguel 1. _____ (have) breakfast at 9 o'clock.
Editor: Okay. How about 10 o'clock?
Agent: Miguel 2. _____ (have) training from 10 until 12.
Editor: Oh. Can we 3. _____ (have) lunch with Miguel at the training ground?
Agent: I'm sorry, Miguel 4. _____ (eat) lunch with his teammates. He needs to make new friends at the club.
Editor: Hmmm. OK. Is Miguel free in the afternoon?
Agent: He 5. _____ (have) training again from 1 to 3. Then he usually 6. _____ (go) shopping with his family. He 7. _____ (have) free time after that, at around 5 o'clock.
Editor: Great. We look forward to speaking to him at 5 tomorrow!

Exercise 2

Describe the daily activities of someone you know. Try to write at least 50 words.
- What do they do? (*Example: She's a professional footballer.*)
- What do they do in the morning / afternoon / evening?
- Do you think their day is busy?

_____
_____
_____
_____
_____
_____

> **Don't forget!**
> Sometimes *they* is used to refer to only one person:
> *They are a professional footballer.*

UNIT 5 | Daily Routine

Reading

Exercise 1

Read the text about players and their daily routines. How many players talk about their matchday kit? ___

GOOD LUCK ON MATCHDAYS

We asked our first-team squad to tell us about their matchday activities. Check out some of their answers…

Luca: I check social media before a match, and I always tweet my fans after we win!

Jack: I wait until we're walking down the tunnel before I put my shirt on.

Harry: I listen to heavy metal music on my way to the stadium. It gives me energy!

Miguel: I always have a shower before starting the warm-up. I don't know why, it's just a habit.

Taka: I always relax the morning before a match by playing FIFA. I like to play as Locomotive London, and I try to beat our matchday opponents!

Liam: I get changed into my lucky underpants ten minutes before the match starts.

Exercise 2

Tick (✓) the activity that each player does first.

Miguel:	☐ shower	☐ warm up	
Luca:	☐ check social media	☐ tweet fans	
Jack:	☐ put shirt on	☐ start to walk down the tunnel	
Harry:	☐ listen to heavy metal music	☐ arrive at the stadium	
Liam:	☐ get changed into lucky underpants	☐ start the match	

Exercise 3

Read Taka's answer again. Answer the questions.

a. Do you play football computer games like FIFA or Pro Evo? If so, which game is your favourite?

_____

b. Do you ever talk about football on social media? Do you follow any football news sites on social media?

_____

UNIT 5 | Daily Routine

My Learning

New Words

New word from Unit 5	Translation

Quick Quiz

- Think of 3 daily activities for the word *have* (*Example: have breakfast*):
  have _____, have _____, have _____
- Find 6 words from this unit to describe your daily routine:
  _____
- What does an *agent* do? Explain their job in your first language.
  _____
  _____
  _____

Reflection

I can understand language to describe daily activities.	☹ 😐 ☺
I can use the correct form of present simple verbs to talk about daily activities.	☹ 😐 ☺
I can understand a short text about matchday routines.	☹ 😐 ☺

In Unit 5, I enjoyed [_____]

I want to know more about [_____]

Choose 2 ways to practise Unit 5:
- ☐ I'll ask people about their daily activities.
- ☐ I'll write 5 sentences about my daily activities this week.
- ☐ I'll read about what my favourite player does on matchdays.
- ☐ My idea: [_____]

REVIEW
Units 1–5

Vocabulary

Exercise 1

a. Put the words below into the correct column.

free kick   penalty box   socks   forward   shoot   ~~pass~~   corner   tackle   defender shorts   gloves   shin pads   halfway line   touchline   kick-off   central midfielder

Player positions	Football verbs	Set pieces	Places on the pitch	Football kit
	pass			

b. Add 1–2 more words you know to each column in the table.

Exercise 2

Read part of an interview with Haruka. Complete the interview with *check*, *have* or *go*.

Interviewer: Do you train the day before a match?

Haruka: Yes, but only a little bit. We ¹. _____ training on Fridays, but it's light. Mostly, we talk about the match on Saturday and how we want to play.

Interviewer: What do you mean by "light" training?

Haruka: Like, for example, we ². _____ to the gym or maybe we do some running. But we don't play a practice match.

Interviewer: I see. So, do you train all day on a Friday?

Haruka: No, we only train in the morning. We usually ³. _____ free time in the afternoon. I ⁴. _____ shopping, or I just ⁵. _____ home early and relax.

Interviewer: What's your matchday routine like?

Haruka: Well, I ⁶. _____ to bed early on a Friday, so I wake up early on a Saturday! I usually get up around 8am. I ⁷. _____ breakfast, ⁸. _____ social media, watch TV, then I go to the stadium...

35

UNITS 1–5 | Review

Vocabulary Building Challenge

UNIT 1 Complete the nationalities.

Argentina: _____

Portugal: _____

Italy: _____

UNIT 2 What's the correct noun for each verb?

Head: _____

Shoot: _____

UNIT 3 Rearrange these letters to make parts of a goal.

rossracb: _____

stop: _____

UNIT 4 Complete the parts of a shirt with vowels.

sl___ ___v___s

b___dg___

c___ll___r

UNIT 5 Think of words connected to…

1. going shopping
_____, _____, _____

2. having a match
_____, _____, _____

Grammar

Exercise 1

Choose the correct word to complete each sentence.

UNIT 1

1. Mbappé *isn't / aren't* from Brazil.
2. Macario *is / are* from the USA.
3. Pedri and Gavi *isn't / aren't* English.

UNIT 2

4. He *shoot / shoots*… It's a goal!
5. You never *pass / passes* the ball!
6. I *cross / crosses* the ball a lot.

UNIT 3

7. *Do / Does* you take penalties?
8. She *take / takes* the penalties.
9. *Do / Does* he score lots of free kicks?

UNIT 4

10. *Who / Whose* are these boots?
11. Are those socks *your / yours*?
12. That's *my / mine* shirt.

UNIT 5

13. We *has / have* a match on Wednesday.
14. She *don't / doesn't* have training today.
15. I *go / goes* shopping after matches.

UNITS 1–5 | Review

Exercise 2

Two friends are talking about Rios' next match. Complete the conversation below with the words from the box.

| are | has | takes | have | mine | Do | pass | scores |

Gabrielle: I've got my ticket for the game on Saturday. Have you got yours?
Marcus: Yeah, I've got 1. _____ too! I can't miss the semi-final!
Gabrielle: 2. _____ you think Rios can win?
Marcus: I don't know. Olímpic Recife 3. _____ a good team.
Gabrielle: Yeah. They 4. _____ the ball so well. And they 5. _____ Roberto. He's the best striker in the country right now. He 6. _____ in almost every game.
Marcus: Yeah. Did you know he 7. _____ 35 goals this season?
Gabrielle: 35? Wow! He 8. _____ great free kicks – he's so dangerous from set pieces...

My Learning

Reflection

How well do you know the vocabulary and grammar from Units 1–5?

Vocabulary					Grammar				
I can describe player positions.		☹	😐	🙂	I can use the correct form of the verb *be*.		☹	😐	🙂
I can use action verbs to describe football.		☹	😐	🙂	I can use the correct form of present simple verbs in the 3rd person.		☹	😐	🙂
I can describe set pieces.		☹	😐	🙂	I can use *do* and *does* correctly to ask questions.		☹	😐	🙂
I can describe places on the pitch		☹	😐	🙂	I can use possessive adjectives.		☹	😐	🙂
I can use the correct verb (*go*, *check*, *have*) with nouns.		☹	😐	🙂					
I can describe items of football equipment.		☹	😐	🙂					

UNIT 6

The Body

Vocabulary

Exercise 1

Put the body parts in the box into the correct columns.

back   arm   ears   hair   shoulder   knee
shin   calf   chest   ankle   nose   eyes
mouth   neck   hamstring   thigh

Head	Body	Legs

Exercise 2

Can you think of a player or someone you know who…

1. had a bad head injury? *Yes*
   Who? / What injury? / When? *Pavard, concussion, Euro 2020*

2. had a serious (very bad) leg injury? _____
   Who? / What injury? / When? _____

3. was injured during a very important match? _____
   Who? / What injury? / Which match? _____

4. is injured right now? _____
   Who? / What injury? / How? _____

5. who was injured but continued to play? _____
   Who? / Which match? / What injury? _____

Vocabulary Building

Exercise 1

We get different types of injuries to different parts of the body. Complete the sentences below with the adjectives from the box.

pulled
sprained
broken

Bones: I have a _____ leg.

Joints (ankles, knees, elbows): She has a _____ ankle.

Muscles: He has a _____ hamstring.

UNIT 6 | The Body

Exercise 2

There's a long injury list at Locomotive London right now! Use the adjectives from Exercise 1 to complete the physio's notes.

Player	Injury	Estimated recovery time	Notes
Miguel	1. _____ calf muscle	2 weeks	Returns to full training tomorrow
Sarah	2. _____ wrist	3 weeks	X-ray yesterday, not broken
Haruka	Two 3. _____ ribs	6 weeks	Rest, no training

Grammar

Exercise 1

a. Rearrange the words to make the questions (**1–5**) in *Ask a ref!*
b. Complete Laura's answers (**A–E**) with a sentence from the box. Not all of the options are needed.

> Yes, you can   No, you can't   Yes, they can   No, they can't

Ask a ref!

We asked Mexican referee Laura Giménez to answer some of your questions about the rules of the game. Over to you, Laura!

1. you / Can / a throw-in / score from ? _____
   A. _____. If your team scores directly from a throw-in, the referee will give a goal kick.

2. from / score / Can / a corner / you ? _____
   B. _____. There's actually a name for this – it's called *an Olimpico*. Meghan Rapinoe scored one in the Olympic Games in 2021!

3. a goal kick / Can / score / you / from ? _____
   C. _____. It's not very common, but it has happened!

4. Can / end / a match / the referee / early ? _____
   D. _____. The referee is the official timekeeper. Sometimes, they end a game early. Sometimes this happens by mistake!

5. a goalkeeper / take / penalties / Can? _____
   E. _____. Do you remember José Luis Chilavert? He once scored 3 penalties in 1 match!

UNIT 6 | The Body

Exercise 2

a. What questions do you have about the rules of the game? Think of 2 questions beginning with *can*. Write them below.

1. _____
2. _____

b. Can you find the answers to your questions online?

Reading

Exercise 1

a. Read part of the commentary from a Locomotive London match. Answer the questions.

1. Who is injured?

   _____

2. What injury do they have?

   _____

3. Can they continue to play in the match?

   _____

4. What problem do Locomotive London have?

   _____

Gabby: Marinha has the ball on the right. She runs down the line. And… oh, she stops.

Diego: It's her hamstring, Gabby.

Gabby: You're right. There were no other players near her. She's holding the back of her leg. Oh, this doesn't look good.

Diego: It's the same leg as last season.

Gabby: Oh dear. Marinha is lying on the ground. The physio comes on. Well, this is really bad luck. Marinha missed 20 games last year with a hamstring injury. She can't carry on.

Diego: She's coming off.

UNIT 6 | The Body

Gabby: The physio signals to the bench. Marinha can't continue.

Diego: She's very upset.

Gabby: Yes, she looks really unhappy. The World Cup starts in 4 weeks. Marinha is Brazil's best player. But it's her left hamstring again. What are your thoughts, Diego?

Diego: Well, there were no other players near her. She's hurt her hamstring. That's it. She's out of the World Cup.

Gabby: Marinha can't walk. She needs to be helped off the pitch. Locomotive London have made all their substitutions. They'll play the last 5 minutes with 10 players on the field...

b. Read the commentary again. Are the sentences true (T) or false (F)?
1. Marinha was injured in a tackle.
2. This isn't the first time Marinha has hurt her hamstring.
3. Marinha is an important player for Brazil.
4. Diego thinks Marinha can't play in the World Cup.
5. Marinha can walk off the pitch.

c. Complete the tweet from a news agency with the words from the box.

hamstring   World Cup   out

Breaking news! Marinha _____ of _____ with _____ injury.

UNIT 6 | The Body

My Learning

New Words

New word from Unit 6	Translation

Quick Quiz

- Name 3 leg injuries a player can get: _____
- Answer this question with a full sentence: Can a defender catch the ball in their penalty box? _____
- What do you call the person who runs onto the pitch to help injured players? _____

Reflection

I can understand language to describe football injuries. ☹ 😐 ☺

I can use *can* and *can't* correctly to describe the rules of football. ☹ 😐 ☺

I can understand a short text about football injuries. ☹ 😐 ☺

In Unit 6, I enjoyed [   ]

I want to know more about [   ]

Choose 2 ways to practise Unit 6:

☐ I'll ask people about the football injuries they've had.
☐ I'll read about the rules in football for dealing with head injuries.
☐ I'll listen for words related to injuries when commentators share team news at the start of a match.
☐ My idea: [   ]

UNIT 7

Describing Players

Vocabulary

Exercise 1

Can you remember the opposite for each word?

fast ← → _____   short ← → _____   big ← → _____
strong ← → _____   overweight ← → _____

Exercise 2

Choose the best option to complete the news headlines.

1. "I'm not *strong / overweight*," says striker seen in fast-food restaurant.
2. Injured in her first game: Is Roberta too *weak / fast* for the Premier League?
3. Manager says 38-year-old defender is "too old and too *tall / slow*".
4. Arsenal 8–0 Village Utd. Arsenal too *strong / slim / weak* for 7th Division team.
5. United fans hope for *big / small / overweight* signings in the transfer window.

Vocabulary Building

Exercise 1

It's London Locomotive v Newcastle Town in a penalty shootout! For penalties **1–5**, draw the movement of the ball from the penalty spot towards the goal.

Example: Locomotive to take first. *Here comes Jack... Oh! It hits the woodwork and goes over!*	1. Can Newcastle take the lead? Here comes Trooper... **Great penalty! Low, bottom right.** 1–0 Newcastle Town.	2. Can Luca level the scores? It's Luca from 12 yards... **Straight down the middle, and into the roof of the net.** 1–1.

43

UNIT 7 | Describing Players

3. Here's Woods for Newcastle. Another great penalty! **He puts the ball into the top left corner.** Newcastle are back in the lead.	4. Up steps Miguel. Oh! That was lucky! **He aims for the top right corner. The ball hits the bar, then the right post, and goes in the net.** Miguel is smiling! It's 2–2.	5. St Martin with Newcastle's third penalty. **No mistake. Bottom left!** It's 3–2.

Grammar

Exercise 1

a. Use these words to write sentences about famous players.

1. Haaland / good finisher: _____
2. Donnarumma / great goalkeeper: _____
3. De Ligt / slow defender: _____
4. Mbappé / good in the air: _____
5. Macario / skilful midfielder: _____
6. Ferran Torres / not good in the air: _____

b. Do you agree with the sentences? Rewrite any sentences you disagree with.

_____
_____

Exercise 2

a. (Circle) any words or phrases in the box that are true for your favourite player.

> good in the air   good on the ball   strong   fast   skilful
>   overweight   tall   two-footed   attacking

b. Write a short paragraph describing your favourite player. Use the words and phrases you've circled to help you.

_____
_____
_____

UNIT 7 | Describing Players

Reading

Exercise 1

Locomotive London want to buy some new players. They're sending their team of scouts around Europe.

Read the scouting report on a player called Carlos Mann. Do the scouting team think he's the right player for Locomotive? Yes / No

Scouting Report

Name: Carlos Mann
Positions: Right back, wing back, right midfield
Age: 29
Club: Borussia Hamburg
Value: 20 million euros

Strengths

- Mann is very fast (100 metres in 11 seconds).
- He's good on the ball.
- He can cross very well. He has 4 assists this season from crosses.
- Mann plays on the right for his club, but he's two-footed.

Weaknesses

- Mann is short. He isn't good in the air.
- His marking from corners and free kicks isn't good.
- He isn't strong. He doesn't defend well against more physical players.

Stats from last match (Borussia Hamburg v Dynamo Munich)

Passes: 101
Pass completion: 93%
Key passes: 2
Tackles: 22
Tackles won: 70%
Crosses: 6
Assists: 1

Verdict

Mann is a good attacking player, but he's weak in defence. He doesn't win enough tackles. Locomotive London need a strong defender. We don't think Mann is the right player for Locomotive.

UNIT 7 | Describing Players

Exercise 2

Read the text again. Complete the table with the words from the box to summarize Carlos Mann's good (+) and bad (–) points.

| height | strength | crossing | marking | tackling | creating chances to score |
| passing | attacking | defending | speed | two-footed | heading |

+	–

Exercise 3

You're a Locomotive London fan. You're discussing Carlos Mann with a friend. How would you respond to their comment?

> I think we should sign Carlos Mann. He's great to watch! I love his runs down the wing – he's an exciting player. He creates goals too...

> True, but _____

My Learning

New Words

New word from Unit 7	Translation

UNIT 7 | Describing Players

Quick Quiz

- Think of 8 adjectives or phrases to describe players:

  _____

- List 4 ways to describe parts or areas of the goal:

  _____

- Explain what a football scout does in your first language:

  _____

Reflection

I can understand language to describe players' skills.	☹ 😐 ☺
I can describe players using *be* + an adjective or football expression.	☹ 😐 ☺
I can understand a short text about scouting.	☹ 😐 ☺

In Unit 7, I enjoyed [_____]

I want to know more about [_____]

Choose 2 ways to practise Unit 7:

☐ I'll describe what I think about a player on social media or in a football forum.

☐ I'll find an old video clip of a penalty shootout and be the commentator.

☐ I'll write my own news headlines about players using language from the unit.

☐ My idea: [_____]

UNIT 8

Playing in a Game

Vocabulary

Exercise 1

Draw lines to match the words together to complete 8 shouts.

play	up
push	off
drop	it
get	it short
hold	side
switch	tight
get goal	the line
clear	it

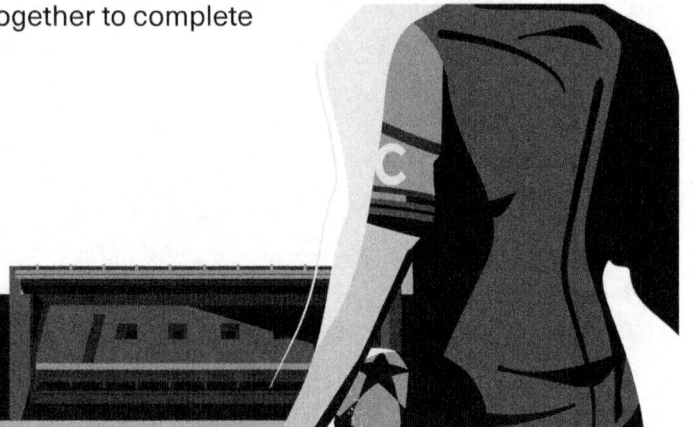

Exercise 2

You're a leader on the pitch! What would you say in each situation?

1. You're defending a corner. Your teammate isn't close enough to one of the attacking players.
   _____

2. You're defending a corner. You head the ball away. You want your teammates to move up the field.
   _____

3. It's a free kick. You want your teammates to stay level. Nobody should drop back too much!
   _____

4. Your teammate gets the ball. No players from the other team are near them, but they don't know that.
   _____

5. Your teammate has the ball. An attacker is running up to them from behind. Your teammate can't see the attacker.
   _____

Vocabulary Building

Exercise 1

Football fans love to shout from the stands too! Match the phrases (**1–5**) with the meanings (**a–e**). You might also hear these phrases on the pitch!

1. Book him/her!	a. That player is in space and has a good chance to score! Pass the ball to them!
2. Come on, ref!	b. That's a great pass/cross!
3. What a ball!	c. Referee, give that player a yellow card!
4. Our ball!	d. I'm not happy with your decision, referee!
5. Play him/her in!	e. The ball touched the other team's player before going out of play.

Exercise 2

You're a Locomotive London fan watching from the stands. What do you shout in these situations?

1. An attacker and a defender jump for a header. They both touch the ball, which goes over the byline. _____

2. Miguel runs between two defenders. If he gets the ball, he'll be one-on-one with the goalkeeper. Jack has the ball. _____

3. The keeper clears the ball 60 yards. It's a perfect pass to the striker.
_____

4. Harry is fouled on the halfway line. The referee says "play on" (continue).
_____

5. A Newcastle Town player fouls Harry on the halfway line. It's his fourth foul of the match already! _____

UNIT 8 | Playing in a Game

Grammar

Exercise 1

Locomotive London captain Lucy is organizing the team to defend a corner. Complete Lucy's shouts with the words and phrases from the box.

> look   mark up   push up   get   don't   stand   watch   get tight

Lucy: Everybody back! Come on! Haruka, 1. _____ walk! OK, 2. _____ !
Who's got number 8? Who's on number 9. I've got number 10.
Marta, Hannah, 3. _____ on the posts!
Mia! 4. _____ ! There's a player coming in!
5. _____ goal-side. Who's on number 7?!
Emma, 6. _____ to Number 7.
EMMA! Tighter! Meghan! 7. _____ the runner!

[The ball comes into the box]

LUCY'S BAAALLL!

[Lucy heads the ball away from the goal]

OUT! 8. _____ ! OUT!

Reading

Exercise 1

Read the conversation from a TV show during matchday. Commentators are sharing updates on different live games. Complete the latest scores:

LOCOMOTIVE LONDON   ___ – ___   MANCHESTER ATHLETIC
NEWCASTLE TOWN   ___ – ___   LIVERPOOL CITY

Jeff: Let's go around the grounds now. I hear there's a goal at Locomotive London. Over to you, Sally.

Sally: Yes, it's Locomotive London nil, Manchester Athletic one. Smith runs at Luca. Luca drops off which gives Smith space to cross. Roberts is unmarked in the centre. He heads the ball into the net from six yards. One–nil Athletic.

UNIT 8 | Playing in a Game

Jeff: Roberts was unmarked! Where was Harry?

Sally: He didn't get tight. This is a problem for Locomotive London today. Defensively they've…

Jeff: Sorry Sally, we'll come back to you. I'm hearing that there's been a goal at Newcastle Town. Diego, what's happening there?

Diego: That's right Jeff! It's now Newcastle Town three, Liverpool City one. Jonny Shelley with the goal. Liverpool push up to the halfway line. The Newcastle keeper plays it long and the Liverpool defence are sleeping. Their line is too high. We know Shelley is fast! He gets to the ball first and shoots first time past Furley. It goes in off the post, three–one.

Sally: Shoot! Yes! Goal Locomotive London! One–one.

Jeff: Unbelievable! It's a goal-fest! Let's go back to Sally…

Exercise 2

Number the events from the TV show in order (**1–5**). When you finish, read the text again to check.

> **Did you know?**
>
> *To equalize* means *to make the scores level/the same*. When a team equalize, we sometimes say that they "are level".

a. Diego describes Newcastle Town's goal. ___
b. Locomotive London equalize. ___
c. Sally starts talking about Locomotive London's defensive problems. ___
d. Sally describes Roberts' goal for Manchester Athletic. ___
e. Jeff stops Sally talking because there is a goal for Newcastle Town. ___

Exercise 3

You're Sally! Describe the Locomotive London goal. Don't forget to mention the goal scorer!

Sally: Shoot! Yes! Goal Locomotive London! One–one.
Jeff: Unbelievable! It's a goal-fest! Let's go back to Sally…
Sally: _____

UNIT 8 | Playing in a Game

My Learning

New Words

New word from Unit 8	Translation

Quick Quiz

- Think of 3 shouts to use when defending a corner or set piece:
  _____

- Think of 3 shouts that include the word *ball*:
  _____

- What other football shouts do you use in your own language?
  _____

Reflection

I can understand language to describe shouts and instructions during a football match.   ☹ 😐 🙂

I can use imperatives correctly when using shouts.   ☹ 😐 🙂

I can understand a short dialogue about live football matches.   ☹ 😐 🙂

In Unit 8, I enjoyed _____

I want to know more about _____

Choose 2 ways to practise Unit 8:

☐ I'll practise the shouts (and my facial expressions!) during a match or in front of the mirror.

☐ I'll watch live matchday coverage of football and listen for language from this unit.

☐ I'll read a *Premier League Team of the Week* article from an English newspaper.

☐ My idea: _____

UNIT 9

After the Game

Grammar

Exercise 1

Complete the article about Liverpool's famous Champions League win with the past simple form of the verbs in brackets.

THE BIGGEST SHOCK EVER?

Some people think Liverpool's Champions League comeback against AC Milan [1] _____ (be) the biggest surprise ever in world football.

AC Milan [2] _____ (be) the favourites to beat Liverpool in the 2005 Champions League final. Milan's team [3] _____ (be) full of superstars. Their striker, Shevchenko, [4] _____ (be) one of the best players in Europe at that time. Midfielder Pirlo [5] _____ (be) very skilful, and defender Maldini [6] _____ (be) perhaps the greatest defender of all time. Liverpool [7] _____ (have) good players too, but not many people believed they could win.

Milan [8] _____ (score) 3 goals in the first half. However, Liverpool [9] _____ (do / not) stop trying. In the second half, they [10] _____ (score) 3 goals in just 6 minutes. This surprised everyone! The game ended 3-3 and went to extra time and penalties.

Milan [11] _____ (miss) their first penalty in the shootout. The Liverpool keeper Dudek [12] _____ (save) two more, including penalties from Pirlo and Shevchenko. Liverpool won the shootout 3-2. Their famous captain, Steven Gerrard, lifted the trophy.

Has there ever been a better final?

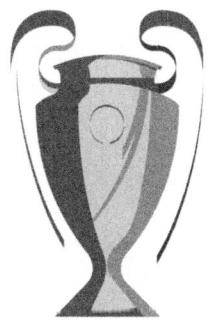

Did you know?

A comeback is when a team is losing but then they draw/win. In a news headline, you might see: *Liverpool comeback shocks AC Milan.*

We also sometimes say, "[Team] *came back* from [score] down to draw/win [score]."

Example: *Liverpool came back from 3-0 down to draw 3-3.*

UNIT 9 | After the Game

Grammar Building

Exercise 1

Translate these verbs into your first language. Then, find the past simple form for each verb in the article above.

Verb	Translation	Past simple
believe		
surprise		
end		
lift (a trophy)		
win (a match)		

Vocabulary

Exercise 1

How many syllables are there in each past simple form? Put the past simple verbs below into the correct column.

~~played~~ passed crossed created headed lifted squared pressed fouled ~~tackled~~ dribbled marked cleared

1 syllable: O	2 syllables: Oo	3 syllables: oOo
played	tackled	

Exercise 2

Complete these famous World Cup moments using words from the box. If you haven't seen these moments, search online for videos to help you.

passed dribbled kicked missed headed crossed dribbled didn't shoot squared tackled

UNIT 9 | After the Game

Harald Schumacher v France — 1982
Schumacher was a goalkeeper. He ¹·_____ a striker very dangerously. The referee only showed him a yellow card.

Diego Maradona v England — 1986
Maradona got the ball near the halfway line. He ²·_____ past 3 or 4 defenders, then he ³·_____ past the goalkeeper and ⁴·_____ the ball in the net.

Roberto Baggio v Brazil — 1994
Baggio ⁵·_____ a penalty in the World Cup final by kicking the ball over the crossbar.

Peter Crouch v Trinidad and Tobago — 2006
The winger ⁶·_____ the ball high in the air. Crouch jumped and ⁷·_____ the ball into the net. The replay showed that Crouch pulled the defender's hair so he could jump higher!

Exercise 3

Can you describe another famous football moment? Try to use at least 2 verbs/phrases from Unit 9. → **Unit 9** Wordlist p84

_____
_____

Reading

Exercise 1

Match the words (**1–4**) with the meanings (**a–d**).

1. hosts	a. something (often bad) that you don't think will happen
2. holders	b. the team who won the last tournament played
3. the favourites	c. the team from the stadium/country where a match/tournament happens
4. shock	d. the team people think will win a tournament

UNIT 9 | After the Game

Exercise 2

Read about the top 3 shock results in football. Complete the sentences.

1. _____ beat _____ in the group stages of the World Cup.
2. _____ beat _____ to win a major tournament.
3. _____ lost by lots of goals.

TOP 3 SHOCK RESULTS IN FOOTBALL

Denmark win Euro 1992
Germany were the favourites to win the 1992 European Championship. At that time, Germany were the World Champions and some of their players were the best of all time.

Germany played Denmark in the final. Denmark surprised everyone when they won the match 2–0.

Brazil concede SEVEN goals
Hosts Brazil played Germany in the 2014 World Cup semi-final in Belo Horizonte. Many people thought Germany would win, but not like this! Germany beat the Brazilian team 7–1. This is Brazil's worst-ever international defeat.

Senegal shock France
Senegal played France in the opening game of World Cup 2002. France were the World Cup holders and the favourites to win the tournament. Incredibly, Senegal won the match 1–0. France then drew and lost their next group games and exited the tournament early. Senegal reached the quarter-finals.

Exercise 3

Read the text again. Which team(s)...

1. were World Champions when they lost a game? _____
2. won a match by more than one goal? _____
3. were playing a match in their own country? _____
4. did better in a tournament than the World Cup holders? _____
5. played each other in the first match of a tournament? _____

Exercise 4

Which of the 3 results do you think is the biggest shock? Explain your answer.

I think _____'s result against _____ was the biggest shock, because _____
_____.

My Learning

New Words

New word from Unit 9	Translation

Quick Quiz

- Think of 3 past simple verbs for football actions:
  _____

- Think of 3 regular past tense verbs ending with the sound /ɪd/:
  _____

- How do you say the words *surprise* and *shock* in your own language?
  _____

Reflection

I can understand language to describe past actions and events in a football match.   ☹ 😐 🙂

I can use the correct form of past simple verbs to describe events.   ☹ 😐 🙂

I can understand a short text about shock results in football.   ☹ 😐 🙂

In Unit 9, I enjoyed [ ]

I want to know more about [ ]

Choose 2 ways to practise Unit 9:
- ☐ I'll describe the events of a match I watch to friends in English.
- ☐ I'll write a match report in English.
- ☐ I'll watch and listen to YouTube clips describing shock results in football (with captions).
- ☐ My idea: [ ]

UNIT 10

Fixtures and Results

Vocabulary

Exercise 1

 the phrases you can use to describe each score. There may be more than one correct answer.

1. **Score: 3-1** three to one — three–one — three and one
2. **Score: 2-2** two and two — two–two — two-all
3. **Score: 0-0** zero–zero — zero to zero — nil–nil
4. **Score: 6-0** six against one — six to nil — six–nil

> **Don't forget!**
> A team **wins** a match. = Locomotive **won** the game.
> A team **beats** another team. = Locomotive **beat** Athletic 8–0.
> A team **loses** a match. = Athletic **lost** the match 8–0.
> A team **loses to** another team. = Athletic **lost to** Locomotive 8–0.

Exercise 2

Choose the correct words to complete the sentences.

1. AC Milan *won / beat* Liverpool in the 2007 Champions League final.
2. Liverpool *won / beat* the Champions League final in 2005.
3. Arsenal *lost / lost to* Barcelona in the 2006 Champions League final.
4. Spurs *lost / lost to* the 2019 Champions League final.
5. Zidane scored when Real Madrid *won / beat* Bayer Leverkusen in the 2002 Champions League final.
6. Chelsea *beat / won to* Man City in the 2021 Champions League final.
7. Gareth Bale scored an overhead kick when Real Madrid *beat / won* the Champions League in 2018.
8. Dortmund *lost to / lost* Bayern in the 2013 Champions League final.

UNIT 10 | Fixtures and Results

Exercise 3

Do you remember any of the Champions League games from Exercise 2? Write your memories of the game.

_____
_____

Vocabulary Building

Exercise 1

Match the words and phrases related to fixtures and results (**1–8**) to the meanings (**a–h**).

1. aggregate score	a. when a match starts later than the kick-off time on the same day
2. (at) home	b. playing at your own ground
3. away	c. a round of games when there are only 8 teams left in a tournament
4. first/second leg	d. the total score across 2 games: 1 played at home, 1 played away
5. knockout game/tournament	e. playing at another team's ground
6. quarter-final	f. 2 matches are played to find a winner
7. delayed	g. a type of game or tournament when the losing team exit the competition
8. semi-final	h. the match before the final

Exercise 2

Complete the sentences with a word or phrase from Exercise 1. Choose the best option.

1. The teams drew 1–1 in the first leg. The home team won the second leg 2–1, so the _____ was 3–2.
2. Palmeiras reached the _____ of the 2021 Copa Libertadores after beating São Paulo in the quarter-final.
3. The match was _____ by 20 minutes.
4. Benfica play their _____ games in red and their _____ games in white.
5. The Coupe de France is a _____ tournament.

UNIT 10 | Fixtures and Results

Grammar

Exercise 1

a. Look at the fixtures for Match Week 8. Explain each fixture in a full sentence using *be + -ing* verb. Include information about whether the team are **at home** or **away**.

Form				Home	Away	Form			
W	D	D	W	Newcastle Town	Leeds Rangers	L	D	D	L
L	L	L	L	Bristol FC	Midlands Villa	W	W	D	W
W	W	D	W	South Coast	Locomotive London	W	L	L	D
W	W	W	W	Norfolk City	Cardiff Central	L	W	L	W
D	D	D	D	Manchester Athletic	Liverpool City	D	D	D	D

Example:
Newcastle Town are playing at home to Leeds Rangers.

1. Midlands Villa are _____ away to _____.
2. South Coast _____.
3. Norfolk City _____.
4. Liverpool City _____.

b. Look at the form guide for each team. This shows the teams' last 4 results. What do the letters mean?

W = _____ **D** = _____ **L** = Loss

c. Based on the form guide, write a prediction for each game about which team will win, lose or draw.

Example:
I think Newcastle Town <u>will beat</u> Leeds.

1. Bristol FC v Midlands Villa:
   _____

2. South Coast v Locomotive London:
   _____

3. Norfolk City v Cardiff Central:
   _____

4. Manchester Athletic v Liverpool City:
   _____

UNIT 10 | Fixtures and Results

Reading

Exercise 1

Read Adam's predictions for transfer deadline day. Choose the correct words to complete the sentences.

1. Adam *thinks / doesn't think* Harry will leave Locomotive.
2. Adam *thinks / doesn't think* Taka will join Manchester Athletic.

Did you know?
European teams can buy players during the pre-season (summer) and January *transfer windows*. The final day of the transfer window is called *transfer deadline day*.

SPORT — **Football**

22:01 Transfer deadline day: 2 hours to go!

The transfer window closes in 2 hours! Ex-England defender Adam shares his views on the latest transfer gossip.

Harry to leave Locomotive?

Adam's views: Harry isn't in the Locomotive starting line-up at the moment. He wants to play for England in the World Cup in the summer, so he needs regular football. Will Locomotive want to sell Harry? I'm not sure. He's only 21 years old and can play well in different positions.

Prediction: I think Harry will stay at Locomotive.

Taka to Manchester Athletic?

Adam's views: Athletic tried to sign Taka in the summer. He'll cost more now, because he's having a brilliant season at Locomotive. Athletic need a full back, but Locomotive won't sell Taka for less than 100 million. Do Athletic have the money?

Prediction: It's too late in the transfer window for a big move like this. I don't think he'll leave.

Exercise 2

Read the text again and answer the questions.

1. Why does Harry need to play for his club team often?
   _____

2. Why will Locomotive want to keep Harry? Give 2 reasons.
   _____, _____

3. How do we know that Manchester Athletic think Taka is a good player?
   _____

4. Why doesn't Adam think Athletic will sign Taka? Give 2 reasons.
   _____, _____

UNIT 10 | Fixtures and Results

Exercise 3

Who do you think your club will sign in the next transfer window? Explain your answer.

I think my club will sign _____, because _____
_____.

My Learning

New Words

New word from Unit 10	Translation

Quick Quiz

- Write the past simple form for these verbs: win – _____, draw – _____, lose – _____

- What grammar form can you use to make predictions in English? _____

- When does the transfer window open in your country? _____

Reflection

I can understand language to describe fixtures and results.	☹ 😐 ☺
I can make predictions about matches using *will* and *won't*.	☹ 😐 ☺
I can understand a short text about transfers.	☹ 😐 ☺

In Unit 10, I enjoyed [_____]

I want to know more about [_____]

Choose 2 ways to practise Unit 10:
- ☐ I'll listen to a preview of the weekend fixtures in English.
- ☐ I'll make predictions about the weekend fixtures in English.
- ☐ I'll read an article (or watch a YouTube video) about predictions for future transfers.
- ☐ My idea: [_____]

REVIEW

Units 6–10

Vocabulary

Exercise 1

Put the words below into the correct column.

~~short~~	crossed	chest	fast	up	off
dribbled	won	hamstring	big	it	ball
shoulder	beat	weak	thigh	drew	passed

Body parts	Opposites	Shouts	Regular past simple verbs	Describing results
_____	tall – _short_	Mark _____!	_____	_____
_____	strong – _____	Easy _____!	_____	_____
_____	_____ – slow	Clear _____!	_____	_____
_____	_____ – small	Drop _____!	_____	_____

Exercise 2

Read the list of results from the weekend fixtures. Complete the summary below with the verbs from the box.

RESULTS

Santa Mineiro	5–0	Rios
Billionaires	0–0	Universidad de la Plata
Sporting Bolívar	1–2	Seniors
Olímpic Recife	0–1	Medellín Old Boys
Deportivo Palmeiras	2–2	Atlético Montevideo
San Sebastián	6–0	Santa Fe City

won
lost to
drew (x2)
beat
lost

There were lots of goals in the South American League this weekend. Santa Mineiro 1._____ Rios 5 0 to stay at the top of the table. Billionaires missed the chance to move into second place when they 2._____ 0–0 with Universidad. Seniors 3._____ away to Sporting Bolívar, with their star player Pedro Clemento scoring in the final minute. Olímpic Recife 4._____ Medellín at home for the first time ever. This means that Olímpic are in the bottom 3. Deportivo 5._____ with Atlético Montevideo after scoring 2 goals in 5 minutes. Santa Fe are still bottom of the league after they 6._____ 6–0 to San Sebastián.

UNITS 6-10 | Review

Grammar

Exercise 1

Complete the sentences by putting the missing word in the correct place.

1. Can score from a goal kick? — *you*
2. Can you be offside from corner? — *a*
3. Konate is strong defender. — *a*
4. Rapinoe good on the ball. — *is*
5. Get side! — *goal*
6. Play short! — *it*
7. She a penalty in the World Cup final. — *missed*
8. He shoot – he passed the ball to his teammate. — *didn't*
9. I think Manchester win 2–1. — *will*
10. City are 10 points behind Athletic. They win the league. — *won't*

Exercise 2

Complete the commentary with the correct form of the verbs in brackets.

C1: It's a corner to Locomotive. Macintyre, the Manchester Athletic captain, is shouting at his teammates to [1]. _____ (mark) up. They have 2 players marking Jack – they know he's good in the air. The cross comes in, and... Macintyre heads it away. Wow, he [2]. _____ (clear) the ball a long way!

C2: Wait. Jack is on the ground in the box. [3]. _____ (be) there some shirt pulling?

C1: It's... The referee blows his whistle and... It's a penalty to Locomotive! Macintyre [4]. _____ (head) the ball clear, but the referee [5]. _____ (see) Gray pull Jack to the ground.

C2: Yes, we can see the replay on the big screen now. The referee is right. It's a foul.

C1: This is a big chance for Miguel. Remember, Miguel [6]. _____ (miss) a penalty last week against Newcastle Town. Locomotive [7]. _____ (lose) that game 1–0. This is a must-win game.

C2: He's going to go down the middle.

C1: Miguel runs to the ball. Can he score from here? No, he [8]. _____ (can / not). He shoots straight down the middle and into the gloves of the goalkeeper.

UNITS 6–10 | Review

Vocabulary and Grammar Building Challenge

UNIT 6 Rearrange these letters to make injuries.	**UNIT 7** Think of 4 places you can aim a penalty.	**UNIT 8** Complete the shouts.
rkenob gel: _____	*Example: straight down the middle*	Come on, _____!
puledl shtamrign: _____	1. _____	Our _____!
denprias ristw: _____	2. _____ 3. _____ 4. _____	

UNIT 9 Complete the past simple forms of the verbs.	**UNIT 10** Complete the sentences.
believe: _____ lift: _____ win: _____	The _____ score is the total score from the first leg and the second leg. If you win the quarter-final, you'll play in the _____.

My Learning

Reflection

How well do you know the vocabulary and grammar from Units 6–10?

Vocabulary					Grammar			
I can describe body parts and injuries.	☹	😐	🙂		I can use *can* and *can't* to describe rules and abilities.	☹	😐	🙂
I can describe players using opposite adjectives.	☹	😐	🙂		I can use the verb *be* with common adjectives to describe players.	☹	😐	🙂
I can understand and use common football shouts.	☹	😐	🙂		I can understand shouts used by players and fans during a match.	☹	😐	🙂
I can use common action verbs in the past simple.	☹	😐	🙂		I can identify the correct form of past simple verbs.	☹	😐	🙂
I can describe scores and results.	☹	😐	🙂		I can use common football verbs (*win*, *lose*, *draw*) in the past simple.	☹	😐	🙂

Grammar Reference

UNIT 1

Present simple *be*

Positive and negative

The verb *be* has 3 forms in the present simple: *am*, *is* and *are*. We make negatives by adding *not* after *be*.

Singular			Plural		
I	am		we	are	
you	are	(not)	you	are	(not)
he / she / it	is		they	are	

Contractions

We often join words together. These joined words are called **contractions**.

Positive (+)			Negative (−)		
I am	→	I'm	I am not	→	I'm not
you are	→	you're	you are not	→	you aren't / you're not
he is	→	he's	he is not	→	he isn't / he's not
she is	→	she's	she is not	→	she isn't / she's not
it is	→	it's	it is not	→	it isn't / it's not
we are	→	we're	we are not	→	we aren't / we're not
they are	→	they're	they are not	→	they aren't / they're not

I'm a midfielder. You're a striker. It's an important match. They're a good team.
I'm not the coach. You aren't a defender. She isn't Brazilian. They're not here yet.

Questions

We make questions by putting the verb *be* before the subject (e.g. *I*, *she*).
We put question words (e.g. *What, Where, Who, When, Why*) at the beginning.

(Question word)	Be	Subject	(Rest of question)
	Am	I	a good player?
	Are	you	ready?
What	is	your name?	
Where	are	the other players?	
Why	are	they	late?
When	is	the match?	

We can also use contractions with question words:
What + is = What's; Where + is = Where's, etc.

What's your name? Where's she from?
When's the match?

Short answers

When somebody asks a *yes/no* question, we often answer with a short answer.

	Positive (+)			Negative (−)	
Yes,	I	am.	No,	I'm	not.
	you / we / they	are.		you / we / they	aren't.
	he / she / it	is.		he / she / it	isn't.

A: *Are you Brazilian?* **B:** *Yes, I am. / No, I'm not.*
A: *Are they defenders?* **B:** *Yes, they are. / No, they aren't.*

UNIT 2

Present simple (+/−)

We use the present simple to talk about:

1. **States** that are true now or always.
   I love football. We want to win the match. She knows the rules.
   State verbs include *like, love, want, know, cost, understand, agree* and *have*.

2. **Actions** that happen always, often, sometimes or never.
   She plays in attack. (= she always plays in that position)
   You often score goals. They sometimes head the ball.

Positive (+)

For most verbs, the present simple is the same as the infinitive. For *he/she/it*, add *-s*.
Two verbs (*be* and *have*) are irregular.

I / you / we / they	play know save have	he / she / it	play**s** know**s** save**s** ha**s**

Spelling: adding *-s* for *he/she/it*

When a verb ends in *-o, -s, -sh, -ch* or *-x*, add *-es*.

I do / go / pass / push / watch / relax → *She does / goes / passes / pushes / watches / relaxes.*

When a verb ends in a consonant (e.g. *d, l, r*) + *y*, change the *-y* to *-ies*.

I study / fly / try. → *He studies / flies / tries.*

> **Did you know?**
>
> *Never* has a negative meaning, but we use it in positive sentences.
>
> *We never win big matches!* (**Not:** ~~We never don't win~~ ...)

Grammar Reference

But when a verb ends in a vowel (*a*, *e*, *i*, *o*, *u*) + *y*, just add *-s*.

I pl*ay* / enj*oy* / b*uy*. → She play*s* / enjoy*s* / buy*s*.

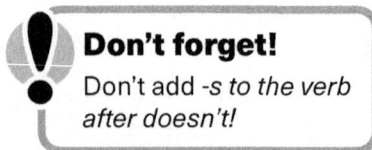

Don't forget!
Don't add *-s* to the verb after *doesn't*!

Negative (–)
We make negatives by adding *don't* (= *do not*) or *doesn't* (= *does not*) before the verb.

I / you / we / they	don't	play know save have	he / she / it	doesn't	play know save have

UNIT 3
Present simple (?)

Yes/no questions
We make *yes/no* questions by adding *do* or *does* before the subject.

Positive				Question			
Subject	**Verb**			***Do/does***	**Subject**	**Verb**	
I You We They	love like hate	football	→	Do	I you we they	love like hate	football?
He She It	loves likes hates			Does	he she it		

Short answers
When somebody asks a *yes/no* question, we often answer with a short answer.

Don't forget!
In questions, don't add *-s* to the verb after *does*!
Does she know the rules?
(**Not:** ~~*Does she knows ...?*~~)

	Positive (+)			Negative (–)	
Yes,	I / you / we / they	do.	No,	I / you / we / they	don't.
	he / she / it	does.		he / she / it	doesn't.

A: *Do you take corners?* **B:** *Yes, I do. / No, I don't.*
A: *Does it hurt when you head the ball?* **B:** *Yes, it does. / No, it doesn't.*

Wh- questions

Wh- questions start with question words like *who*, *what*, *where*, *when*, *why* and *how*, or phrases like *what time*, *how often* or *which position*.

Question word/phrase	Do/does	Subject		Verb	
Where	does	she		play?	
Why	do	they	always	win?	
What time	does	your training		start	on Tuesdays?
Which position	do	you		play	in?

Subject questions

When you ask about the subject, the word order is the same as in a positive sentence. Don't add *do/does*.

Positive				Subject question		
Subject	Verb			Question word/phrase	Verb	
Emma	passes	the most.	→	Who	passes	the most?
Liam	takes	penalties.		Which player	takes	penalties?
Something	happens	after a foul.		What	happens	after a foul?

UNIT 4

Possessives

Possessives with apostrophe + *-s*

We use possessives to show that something belongs to somebody. We usually do this by adding an apostrophe (') and *-s* after the person.

> This ball belongs to Kevin. It's <u>Kevin's</u> ball. The ball is <u>Kevin's</u>.
> These boots belong to the player in the red shirt. They're <u>the player in the red shirt's</u> boots.

> **Did you know?**
>
> When there's already an *-s* to show a plural (e.g. *the 3 defender<u>s</u>*), just add an apostrophe after the *-s*. Don't add another *-s*.
>
> These shirts belong to the 3 defenders. They're the 3 defender<u>s</u>' shirts.

Possessive determiners and possessive pronouns

We use possessive determiners (e.g. *my*) **before** a noun. We use possessive pronouns (e.g. *mine*) **instead of** a noun.

> These socks belong to me. They're <u>my</u> socks. These socks are <u>mine</u>.

Personal pronoun	Possessive determiner	Possessive pronoun
I	They're **my** socks.	They're **mine**.
you	They're **your** socks.	They're **yours**.
he	They're **his** socks.	They're **his**.
she	They're **her** socks.	They're **hers**.
it	They're **its** socks.	–
we	They're **our** socks.	They're **ours**.
they	They're **their** socks.	They're **theirs**.
who	**Whose** socks are they?	**Whose** are these socks?

Singular and plural
We use singular forms (e.g. *a ball*, *a player*) for one person or thing, and plural forms (e.g. *balls*, *players*) for more than one person or thing.

We use *a* or *an* before a noun to show that it's singular. Use *a* before a consonant sound: *a ball*, *a goal*. Use *an* before a vowel sound: *an attacker*, *an open goal*.

We usually use *-s* after a noun to show that it's plural: *10 balls, 22 players, 2 attackers*.

This, *that*, *these* and *those*
We use *this* for something that's "here" (= near the speaker) and *that* for something that's "there" (= away from the speaker). The plural forms are *these* and *those*.

	Singular	Plural
"here"	this	these
"there"	that	those

This shirt (here) is red; that shirt (there) is blue.
These socks (here) are white; those socks (there) are green.

UNIT 5

Present simple for routines
We use the present simple to talk about our daily routines (= things we do every day).

Adverbs of frequency
We use adverbs of frequency to say how often something happens.

0%				100%
never	not often	sometimes	often/usually	always

Most adverbs of frequency come after *be* and *not* (or *n't*), but before other verbs.

A: *You never pass to me.*   **B:** *You're never in the right place for me to pass to you!*
We usually lose our matches and it's usually my fault.
She doesn't always score a goal because she isn't always a striker.

Grammar Reference

Frequency expressions

We use frequency expressions to say **exactly** how often something happens.

I play football	every		morning / afternoon / evening. day. Sunday / Tuesday / Thursday. week. month.
	once twice three times ten times	a every	day. week. month.

Time expressions with prepositions

We use *at* with times: *at ten o'clock, at midnight*.

We use *on* for days: *on Tuesdays*.

We use *in* with parts of a day:
in the morning(s), in the afternoon(s), in the evening(s).
But we use *at* with *night*: *at night*.

We use *in* with months, seasons, years, etc.:
in July, in the spring, in 2023.

> **Did you know?**
> In British English, people say "**at** the weekend(s)". In American English, people say "**on** (the) weekend(s)".

UNIT 6

Can

Positive and negative

We use *can* to talk about ability, rules and permission. The negative form is *can't* (= *can* + *not*).

Positive (+)			Negative (−)		
I / you / he / she / it / we / they	can	play football.	I / you / he / she / it / we / they	can't	play football.

Ability: *I can't score a goal from the halfway line – it's too far!*
Rules: *The goalkeeper can use his or her hands, but the other players can't pick it up.*
Permission: *No, sorry, you can't play in attack today. We need you in defence.*

> **Don't forget!**
> With *can*, there's no *-s* for *he/she/it*: *He can play.*
> (**Not:** ~~He cans play.~~)
>
> There's no *to* after *can*:
> *We can't run fast.*
> (**Not:** ~~We can't to run fast.~~)

Questions

We make questions by putting the verb *can* before the subject.

(Question word/phrase)	Can/can't	Subject	Verb	
	Can	you	play	in goal?
Why	can't	I	keep	playing?
When	can	the match	start?	
Which positions	can	she	play	in?

 Don't forget!
Subject questions have the same word order as positive sentences.
Lucy can dribble the ball the best. → *Which player can dribble the ball the best?*

Short answers

When somebody asks a question with *can*, we often answer with a short answer.

	Positive (+)			Negative (–)	
Yes,	I / you / he / she / it / we / they	can.	No,	I / you / he / she / it / we / they	can't.

A: *Can you move your arm?* **B:** *Yes, I can. / No, I can't.*
A: *Can I take this corner, please?* **B:** *Yes, you can. / No, you can't.*

UNIT 7

Be + adjective/football expressions

Be + adjective

We often use *be* + adjective to describe somebody or something.

I'm tired. It's difficult. They're excellent.

 Don't forget!
There are 3 forms of *be* in the present simple: *I am; you/we/they are; he/she/it is.*

You can use *very* or *really* to make the meaning of the adjective stronger. Use *quite* to make it weaker. Use *not very* to make it very weak.

strong ◄──────────────────────────────► **weak**

She's very/really good.   *She's good.*   *She's quite good.*   *She isn't very good.*

Be (+ adjective) + noun

We can also use *be* + noun to describe somebody or something. We can add 1 or more adjectives before the noun. We can add words like *very*, *really* and *quite* before the adjective.

He's a defender.   *He's a skilful, left-footed defender.*
He's a left-footed defender.   *He's a really skilful, left-footed defender.*

Grammar Reference

 Don't forget!
We use *a/an* to show that the noun is singular and *-s* to show it's plural.
They're defenders.
(**Not:** *They're a defenders.*)

Did you know?
Opinion adjectives (e.g. *good, skilful, fast, tall*) come before fact adjectives (e.g. *right-footed*).
She's a good, two-footed midfielder.
(**Not:** *She's a two-footed good midfielder.*)

Be + adjective + expression
We can sometimes add expressions after *be* + adjective.

Subject + *be*	Adjective	Expression
I'm	excellent	**on** the ball.
You're	good	**at** football / passing / defending.
She's	not bad	**with** her head / left foot.
	not very good	
He's	terrible	**in** the air / in attack / in midfield.

So and *such*
We can use *so* and *such* to make an adjective stronger. Use *so* when there's an adjective without a noun. Use *such* when there's an adjective and a noun.
He's so skilful. He's such a skilful player.

UNIT 8

Imperatives

Basic imperatives
We use imperatives to ask or tell other people what to do. They have the same form as the infinitive of the verb (e.g. *be, go, wait*).

Be careful!
Go back!
Wait for me!

Negative imperatives
Negative imperatives start with *don't*.

Don't touch the ball!
Don't tell me what to do!
Don't be so rude!

Polite imperatives
Imperatives sometimes sound rude. You can add *please* to make them sound more polite.

Please wait here.
Follow me, please.

Did you know?
You can also use *can* instead of an imperative to ask somebody to do something.
Can you come here, please?
Can you say that again, please?

Grammar Reference

Imperatives for more than one person

You can use a phrase like *you two*, *all of you* or *everybody* to make it clear that an imperative is for more than one person.

All of you be quiet!
OK, everybody listen to me.
Stop fighting, you two.

UNIT 9

Past simple

Be

The verb *be* has 2 forms in the past simple: *was* and *were*. The negative forms are *wasn't* (= *was not*) and *weren't* (= *were not*).

Positive (+)			Negative (−)		
I / He / She / It	was	good.	I / He / She / It	wasn't	good.
We / You / They	were		We / You / They	weren't	

It wasn't a good match. We were terrible.
The score was 4–0. All the players were sad.

To make a *yes/no* question, put *was/were* before the subject.

Question			Short answer		
Was	I / he / she / it	good?	Yes,	I / he / she / it	was.
			No,		wasn't.
Were	you / we / they	good?	Yes,	you / we / they	were.
			No,		weren't.

A: *Were you happy with the result?* **B:** *No, we weren't.*
A: *Was the referee fair?* **B:** *Yes, she was.*

To make a *wh-* question, put a question word or phrase before *was/were*.

What was the score? Why were the players sad?

Regular verbs

To make the past simple form of regular verbs, add *-ed*. To make the negative form, use *didn't* (= *did not*) + infinitive.

Positive (+)			Negative (−)			
I / You / He / She / It / We / They	played	well.	I / You / He / She / It / We / They	didn't	play	well.
	scored	a goal.			score	a goal.
	headed	the ball.			head	the ball.

Grammar Reference

To make a *yes/no* question, put *did* before the subject and put the infinitive after the subject.

	Question				Short answer	
Did	I / you / he / she / it / we / they	play	well?	Yes,	I / you / he / she / it / we / they	did.
		score	a goal?	No,		didn't.

Don't forget!
After *did* and *didn't*, the verb is in the infinitive, not the past simple:
Did you play well?
(**Not:** *Did you played well?*)
We didn't play well.
(**Not:** *We didn't played well.*)

To make a *wh-* question, put a question word or phrase before *did*.

Where did you play? Who did you play against? What time did the match start?

Don't forget!
Subject questions have the same word order as positive sentences.
Miguel scored a goal. → Who scored a goal?

Spelling regular verbs

For most regular verbs, add *-ed*.

head → head<u>ed</u>, miss → miss<u>ed</u>

When the verb already ends in *-e*, just add *-d*.

sav<u>e</u> → save<u>d</u>, agre<u>e</u> → agree<u>d</u>

When the verb ends in a consonant (e.g. *p, r*) + *-y*, change the *-y* to *-ied*.

cop<u>y</u> → cop<u>ied</u>, tr<u>y</u> → tr<u>ied</u>

But when the verb ends in a vowel (*a, e, i, o, u*) + *-y*, just add *-ed*.

pla<u>y</u> → play<u>ed</u>, enjo<u>y</u> → enjoy<u>ed</u>

When the verb ends in one vowel + one consonant, double the consonant.

pl<u>an</u> → pla<u>nned</u>, st<u>op</u> → sto<u>pped</u>

Grammar Reference

Irregular verbs

Many verbs are irregular in the past simple. That means you can't simply add -ed to make the past simple. You need to learn the past form. See page 95 for a list of irregular verbs.

We won the match.
She shot 3 times but didn't score!

UNIT 10

Future tense

Future tense (*will*)

We use *will* to make predictions about the future. The negative form is *won't* (= *will not*).

Positive (+)			Negative (−)		
I / You / He / She / It / We / They	will	win.	I / You / He / She / It / We / They	won't	win.

We often use contractions with *will*: *I'll* (= *I will*), *you'll*, *he'll*, *she'll*, *it'll*, *we'll*, *they'll*; *won't* (= *will not*).

We won't win. They'll probably beat us 10–0!

> **Did you know?**
> We often use the phrase *I don't think* to make negatives with *will*.
> *I don't think we'll win.*

To make a *yes/no* question, put *will* before the subject. To make a *wh-* question, put a question word or phrase before *will*.

Question			Short answer		
Will	I / you / he / she / it / we / they	win?	Yes,	I / you / he / she / it / we / they	will.
			No,		won't.

A: *Will you score a goal?* **B:** *Yes, I will.*

How many goals will they score?

> **Did you know?**
> We often use the phrase *do you think* to make questions with *will*. When we use *do you think*, we put *will* after the subject.
>
> **A:** *Do you think you'll score a goal?*
> (**Not:** *Do you think will you score a goal?*)
>
> **B:** *Yes, I do.* (**Not:** *Yes, I will.*)
> *How many goals do you think they'll score?*

Be + *-ing* verb for future

We use a present form of the verb *be* + the *-ing* form of a verb (e.g. *playing*) to talk about future fixtures and plans.

I'm playing in goal tomorrow because our goalkeeper is injured.
We bought a new striker last week. She's starting with us tomorrow.
We aren't playing next week because it's a holiday weekend.
A: *Am I playing tomorrow?* **B:** *Yes, you are. / No, you aren't.*
Who are we playing on Thursday?

Don't forget!
There are 3 forms of *be* in the present simple: *I am; you/we/they are; he/she/it is.*

Irregular Verbs

Infinitive	Past Simple	Past Participle
be	was / were	been
beat	beat	beaten
become	became	become
begin	began	begun
bring	brought	brought
buy	bought	bought
catch	caught	caught
choose	chose	chosen
come	came	come
cost	cost	cost
do	did	done
draw	drew	drawn
drink	drank	drunk
drive	drove	driven
eat	ate	eaten
fall	fell	fallen
feel	felt	felt
find	found	found
fly	flew	flown
forget	forgot	forgotten
get	got	got
give	gave	given
go	went	gone
have	had	had
hear	heard	heard
hit	hit	hit
hold	held	held
hurt	hurt	hurt
keep	kept	kept
know	knew	known
leave	left	left
let	let	let
lose	lost	lost
make	made	made
mean	meant	meant
meet	met	met
pay	paid	paid
put	put	put
read	read	read
ride	rode	ridden
run	ran	run
say	said	said
see	saw	seen
sell	sold	sold
send	sent	sent
shoot	shot	shot
sing	sang	sung
sit	sat	sat
sleep	slept	slept
speak	spoke	spoken
spend	spent	spent
stand	stood	stood
steal	stole	stolen
swim	swam	swum
take	took	taken
teach	taught	taught
tell	told	told
think	thought	thought
throw	threw	thrown
understand	understood	understood
wake	woke	woken
wear	wore	worn
win	won	won
write	wrote	written

Wordlists

UNIT 1

central midfielder (n)	/ˈsentrəl ˌmɪdˈfiːldə(r)/	A central midfielder runs from box to box.
centre back (n)	/ˌsentə ˈbæk/	Centre backs are usually tall.
centre forward (n)	/ˌsentə ˈfɔːwəd/	Centre forwards wear the number 9 shirt.
coach (n)	/kəʊtʃ/	A coach helps the players get better at football.
defender (n)	/dɪˈfendə(r)/	Defenders stop the other team from scoring.
forward (n)	/ˈfɔːwəd/	A forward's job is to score goals.
full back (n)	/ˈfʊl bæk/	Full backs play on the sides of the defence.
goalkeeper (n)	/ˈgəʊlkiːpə(r)/	A goalkeeper saves the ball.
midfielder (n)	/ˌmɪdˈfiːldə(r)/	Midfielders play in the middle of the pitch.
position (n)	/pəˈzɪʃn/	Pele's position was a forward.
winger (n)	/ˈwɪŋə(r)/	Wingers are usually fast and good at dribbling.

UNIT 2

clear (v)	/klɪə(r)/	The defender cleared the ball off the line to stop a goal.
cross (v)	/krɒs/	The winger crossed the ball for the forward to score a goal.
head (v)	/hed/	Defenders jump high to head the ball away.
mark (v)	/mɑːk/	Defenders mark forwards closely at corners and free kicks.
pass (v)	/pɑːs/	Midfielders pass the ball to the forwards so they can score.
save (v)	/seɪv/	The goalkeeper has saved the penalty!
shoot (v)	/ʃuːt/	Forwards shoot a lot.
tackle (v)	/ˈtækl/	Defenders tackle forwards to get the ball from them.

UNIT 3

box (n)	/bɒks/	Most goals are scored inside the box.
centre circle (n)	/ˈsentə(r) ˈsɜːkl/	Only one team can go inside the centre circle at kick-off.
corner (n)	/ˈkɔːnə(r)/	The ball is usually crossed into the box from a corner.
corner flag (n)	/ˈkɔːnə(r) flæg/	A corner is taken from next to the corner flag.
free kick (n)	/ˌfriː ˈkɪk/	A foul outside the box is a free kick.
goal (n) (*action*)	/gəʊl/	She's scored 40 goals this season.
goal (n) (*place*)	/gəʊl/	The goalkeeper stands in the goal.
goal kick (n)	/ˈgəʊl kɪk/	Goalkeepers can kick the ball really far from goal kicks.
halfway line (n)	/ˌhɑːfˈweɪ laɪn/	Everybody must stand behind the halfway line at kick-off.
kick-off (n)	/ˈkɪk ɒf/	Kick-off is at 8pm.
penalty (n)	/ˈpenəlti/	A foul inside the box is a penalty.
set piece (n)	/ˌset ˈpiːs/	Free kicks, corners and throw-ins are examples of set pieces.
throw-in (n)	/ˈθrəʊɪn/	When the ball goes off the side of the pitch, it's a throw-in.
touchline (n)	/ˈtʌtʃlaɪn/	The referee's assistant runs up and down the touchline.

UNIT 4

black (adj)	/blæk/	Referees usually wear black.
blue (adj)	/bluː/	Italy and France wear blue shirts.
boot (n)	/buːt/	You wear boots on your feet to play football.
glove (n)	/glʌv/	Goalkeepers wear gloves on their hands.
green (adj)	/griːn/	The pitch is green.
hat (n)	/hæt/	Goalkeepers sometimes wear a hat if it's sunny.
kit (n)	/kɪt/	Your kit is all the things you wear to play football.
orange (adj)	/ˈɒrɪndʒ/	The Netherlands wear orange shirts.

shin pad (n)	/ˈʃɪnpæd/	You wear shin pads under your socks to stop your legs getting hurt.
shirt (n)	/ʃɜːt/	Every team has their own shirt. It sometimes has your name and number on the back.
shorts (n)	/ʃɔːts/	Every player wears shorts in a match. They keep your legs cool while you're playing.
sock (n)	/sɒk/	You put socks on your feet before you put on your shoes.
tracksuit (n)	/ˈtræksuːt/	You wear a tracksuit before a game.
white (adj)	/waɪt/	Real Madrid have a white shirt.
yellow (adj)	/ˈjeləʊ/	Brazil are the most famous team to wear yellow.

UNIT 5

check social media (phr)	/tʃek ˈsəʊʃl ˈmiːdiə/	Many players check social media after a match to read messages from friends.
eat lunch (phr)	/iːt lʌntʃ/	It's important to eat a healthy lunch after training.
go home (phr)	/gəʊ həʊm/	Professional players usually go home after they finish training.
go shopping (phr)	/gəʊ ˈʃɒpɪŋ/	I go shopping at the supermarket to buy food.
go to bed (phr)	/gəʊ tə bed/	Football players should go to bed early.
go to sleep (phr)	/gəʊ tə sliːp/	I go to sleep at 10pm.
go to the gym (phr)	/gəʊ tə ðə dʒɪm/	I go to the gym so I can get stronger.
have a match (phr)	/hæv ə mætʃ/	We have a match on Saturday at 3pm.
have breakfast (phr)	/hæv ˈbrekfəst/	She has breakfast at 8:30am at the training ground.
have dinner (phr)	/hæv ˈdɪnə(r)/	He has dinner at 7pm with his family.
have free time (phr)	/hæv friː taɪm/	Professional players usually have free time in the afternoon.
have training (phr)	/hæv ˈtreɪnɪŋ/	Professional players usually have training in the morning.
use my phone (phr)	/juːz maɪ fəʊn/	I use my phone to take photos, listen to music and chat with friends.
wake up (phr)	/weɪk ʌp/	I wake up early – at 6am.

UNIT 6

ankle (n)	/ˈæŋkl/	Ouch! I think I sprained my ankle!
arm (n)	/ɑːm/	Defenders use their arms to hold off attackers.
back (n)	/bæk/	My name and number are on my back.
calf (n)	/kɑːf/	I can't walk – I think I pulled my calf!
chest (n)	/tʃest/	Good players use their chest to control the ball in the air.
ear (n)	/ɪə(r)/	Use your ears to listen to the coach!
eye (n)	/aɪ/	Referees need good eyes so they can see everything happening quickly in the game.
foot (n)	/fʊt/	Do you like to kick with your left foot or your right foot?
hair (n)	/heə(r)/	Ronaldinho had long hair, but Zidane had no hair!
hamstring (n)	/ˈhæmstrɪŋ/	She's pulled her hamstring. She can't play for 6 weeks.
head (n)	/hed/	He used his head to score from a high cross.
knee (n)	/niː/	He injured his knee. He might not play again this year.
leg (n)	/leg/	My legs are very tired after a match.
mouth (n)	/maʊθ/	In a game, open your mouth and shout to your teammates.
neck (n)	/nek/	I hurt my neck, so I can't turn my head.
nose (n)	/nəʊz/	He kicked me in the face and broke my nose. It was a clear red card!
shin (n)	/ʃɪn/	It really hurts if you get kicked in the shin!
shoulder (n)	/ˈʃəʊldə(r)/	It wasn't handball – it hit my shoulder!
thigh (n)	/θaɪ/	Your thigh is the part of the leg above the knee.

UNIT 7

big (adj)	/bɪg/	Barça v Real Madrid is a big game.
fast (adj)	/fɑːst/	Mbappé is very fast.
good in the air (adj)	/gʊd ɪn ði eə(r)/	Centre backs are good in the air.
good on the ball (adj)	/gʊd ɒn ðə bɔːl/	Central midfielders need to be good on the ball.

left-footed (adj)	/left ˈfʊtɪd/	Left-footed players kick the ball better with their left foot.
overweight (adj)	/ˌəʊvəˈweɪt/	Overweight players are too heavy. It's hard to run if you're overweight.
right-footed (adj)	/raɪt ˈfʊtɪd/	Right-footed players kick the ball better with their right foot.
short (adj)	/ʃɔːt/	Maradona was short. He was only 165cm.
skilful (adj)	/ˈskɪlfl/	Skilful players control the ball well and are good at dribbling.
slim (adj)	/slɪm/	Professional footballers should be slim, not overweight.
slow (adj)	/sləʊ/	It's hard for slow defenders to play against fast forwards.
small (adj)	/smɔːl/	Uruguay is the smallest country to win a World Cup. Their population is only 3.5 million.
strong (adj)	/strɒŋ/	Centre backs need to be strong.
tall (adj)	/tɔːl/	Professional goalkeepers are usually tall. Their average height in the Premier League is 190cm.
weak (adj)	/wiːk/	Weak players are easily pushed off the ball.

UNIT 8

clear it (phr)	/klɪə(r) ɪt/	Clear it! It's the 90th minute – just get the ball away from the goal.
drop off (pv)	/drɒp ɒf/	Defence, drop off to the edge of the box! Our line is too high.
get tight (phr)	/get taɪt/	Get tight! Don't give them any space!
hold the line (phr)	/həʊld ðə laɪn/	When the other team have a free kick, we need to hold the line. Don't drop off into the box!
keep the ball (phr)	/kiːp ðə bɔːl/	Keep the ball! Don't just kick it back to the other team!
man on (phr)	/mæn ɒn/	Shout "man on" to your teammate when they can't see a player from the other team coming from behind them.
play it long (phr)	/pleɪ ɪt lɒŋ/	Play it long! There's lots of space behind their defence.

Wordlists

play it short (phr)	/pleɪ ɪt ʃɔːt/	Play it short! We need to keep the ball.
push up (pv)	/pʊʃ ʌp/	After we clear the ball, the defence needs to push up. Keep the other team away from our goal!
shoot (v)	/ʃuːt/	We need goals, so we need to shoot more.
switch it (phr)	/swɪtʃ ɪt/	Switch it! There's so much space on the left side of the pitch!
time (v)	/taɪm/	Time! There's nobody near you!

UNIT 9

create a chance (phr)	/kriˈeɪt ə tʃɑːns/	Players like Zidane and Cruyff created many chances to help their teams score goals.
dribble (v)	/ˈdrɪbl/	Wingers like to dribble the ball at the opposite full back.
head (v)	/hed/	Defenders try to head the ball away from corners and free kicks.
pass to (the midfielder) (phr)	/pɑːs tə (ðə ˌmɪdˈfiːldə(r))/	The best goalkeepers don't just clear it – they pass to the midfielders or defenders.
press the defence (phr)	/pres ðə dɪˈfens/	Pep Guardiola's and Jurgen Klopp's teams are very good at winning the ball back by pressing the defence of the other team.
score a penalty (phr)	/skɔː(r) ə ˈpenəlti/	Ronaldo scored a penalty after their defender handballed it in the box.
square (v)	/skweə(r)/	We square the ball to find a little space for our teammate in midfield or in the box.
switch (v)	/swɪtʃ/	We need to switch the ball from left to right so we can find more space.

UNIT 10

beat (v)	/biːt/	Wingers try to beat the full back so they can cross the ball into the box.
bottom (n)	/ˈbɒtəm/	The worst team in the league is at the bottom.
draw (v)	/drɔː/	Senegal drew one–one (1–1) with Cameroon.
fifth (det; adv)	/fɪfθ/	Gamba Osaka are fifth (5th) in the J-League.
fixture (n)	/ˈfɪkstʃə(r)/	We have a difficult fixture this weekend: we're away at Manchester!
fourth (det; adv)	/fɔːθ/	Cerezo Osaka are fourth (4th) in the J-League.
lose (v)	/luːz/	We can't lose to Liverpool City. They're terrible!
nil (n)	/nɪl/	We drew with South Korea nil–nil (0–0).
result (n)	/rɪˈzʌlt/	North Macedonia beat Italy one–nil (1–0) in Palermo. That's an amazing result!
second (det; adv)	/ˈsekənd/	Morocco finished second (2nd) in their group, so they'll go through to the next round.
third (det; adv)	/θɜːd/	Thailand finished third (3rd) in their group, so they won't go through.
top (n)	/tɒp/	The best team in the league is at the top.
win (v)	/wɪn/	Real Madrid have won the Champions League the most times.

Answer Key

UNIT 1
VOCABULARY
Exercise 1

Sarah: 1
Hannah: 3
Marta: 2
Lucy: 5 (c)
Kim: 4
Emma: 6
Haruka: 8
Rachel: 7
Meghan: 10
Mia: 9
Yuna: 11

Exercise 2

Your own answers

VOCABULARY BUILDING
Exercise 1

1. What's your phone number?
2. What's your email address?
3. Do you use WhatsApp?
4. Are you on Instagram?
5. Can I add you on Facebook?
6. Do you follow Marcus Rashford on Twitter?

Exercise 2

a. 1. Argentina, Argentinian. Example answer: Lionel Messi
   2. Portugal, Portuguese. Example answer: Ronaldo
   3. South Korea, South Korean. Example answer: Son Heung-Min
   4. Italy, Italian. Example answer: Sara Gama
   5. Your own answers
   6. Your own answers
b. 1. Portuguese, Portugal
   2. the USA, American
   3. Algerian, Algeria
   4. Spain, Spanish

GRAMMAR
Exercise 1

1. is
2. isn't
3. is
4. are
5. are (*is* can be used in American English)
6. is
7. is

Exercise 2

1. Is
2. 're/are
3. isn't/is not
4. Are
5. 're/are
6. 's/is
7. 's/is

Exercise 3

1. What's / What is your name?
2. Where are you from?
3. How old are you?
4. What's / What is your position? / What position do you play?
5. Who's / Who is your favourite player?

READING
Exercise 1

No. (Jack is a defender, but he already plays for Locomotive London.)

Exercise 2

1. Roberto (40 caps for Brazil); Alex Danger (the captain of Belgium)
2. Roberto (can play as a winger); Vincent (is a winger).
3. Harry and Jack
4. Vincent Danger (Vincent is available for free after leaving Sporting Madrid.)
5. Harry (is unhappy because he isn't playing every game).

Answer Key

Exercise 3
a. Your own answers
b. Your own answers

UNIT 2
VOCABULARY
Exercise 1

Defence: mark, clear, save
Attack: shoot, cross
Both: head (we head clear, we also head towards goal), pass (we might pass back to the goalkeeper to clear, or pass forwards when attacking), tackle (a defender might tackle a forward, and a forward might tackle a defender to win the ball so they can shoot)

Exercise 2

a. Example answers – your drawings might look different!

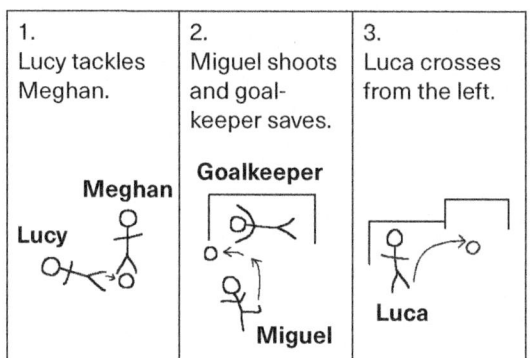

1. Lucy tackles Meghan.
2. Miguel shoots and goalkeeper saves.
3. Luca crosses from the left.

b. Your own answers

VOCABULARY BUILDING
Exercise 1

a. pass (v), pass (n)
cross (v), cross (n)
shoot (v), shot (n)
head (v), header (n)
clear (v), clearance (n)

b. 1. shot
2. header
3. clearance/save
4. pass/cross
5. tackle

GRAMMAR
Exercise 1

a. 2. doesn't pass
3. passes
4. shoot
5. tackles
6. marks
7. don't see
8. Does
9. 're/are
10. cross
11. take
12. takes

b. 1. isn't
2. isn't
3. shoots
4. crosses
5. helps

READING
Exercise 1

a. 1–0 (to Manchester Athletic)
b. Silamino gets a red card for handball.

Exercise 2

1. False: Luca fouls Brown, not Silamino.
2. True: Harry is near the penalty spot.
3. False: Michael scores with his head.
4. False: Miguel takes corners.
5. False: Silamino uses his hand to stop Jack's header.

Exercise 3

Your own answers

UNIT 3
VOCABULARY
Exercise 1

Set piece: throw-in, kick-off, free kick, penalty, corner, goal kick
Place on a football pitch: halfway line, touchline, centre circle, penalty box

Exercise 2

a. 1c; 2a; 3e; 4d; 5b
b. 2. It's a goal kick.
3. It's a corner.
4. It's a penalty.
5. It's a throw-in.

Answer Key

VOCABULARY BUILDING
Exercise 1

a. 1. byline
   2. crossbar
   3. post
   4. penalty spot
b. Suggested answers:
   2. Penalty, yellow/red card
   3. Yellow/red card, maybe a free kick or penalty
   4. Penalty, red card
   5. Corner
   6. Yellow card

GRAMMAR
Exercise 1

1. takes
2. take
3. take
4. takes
5. takes
6. takes
7. Does
8. misses

Exercise 2

Your own answers

READING
Exercise 1

1. win
2. set pieces

Exercise 2

1. away – home
2. goal – free
3. central midfielders – centre backs
4. free kicks – penalties
5. plays – doesn't play
6. never – often

Exercise 3

Suggested answers: set pieces, free kicks, corners, (long) throw-ins, penalties, set-piece taker, take free kicks / corners / penalties

UNIT 4
VOCABULARY
Exercise 1

1. headband
2. gloves
3. shirt
4. shorts
5. socks
6. boots

Exercise 2

2. blue, red
3. green, white
4. red, black
5. yellow
6. orange

VOCABULARY BUILDING
Exercise 1

1. collar
2. stripes
3. sleeves
4. badge

Exercise 2

1. Juventus/Udinese
2. Real Madrid
3. True: They play in dark red (burgundy) and blue.
4. White (Arsenal play in red shirts with white sleeves.)
5. Borussia Dortmund
6. France (a cockerel), Germany (an eagle)

READING
Exercise 1

1. Kit Manager
2. kit / players' kit / equipment

Exercise 2

1. True: She has lunch at the staff café.
2. False: She has an assistant (Dave).
3. False: She hangs them on the locker doors.
4. True: He changes his socks.
5. False: He wears white/purple tape for home matches to match the Locomotive London home shirts.

Answer Key

Exercise 3

Your own answers

GRAMMAR
Exercise 1

1. Whose
2. yours
3. mine
4. my
5. his
6. your
7. mine
8. This
9. Their
10. yours

Exercise 2

1. That red shirt is yours.
2. Those purple shin pads are yours.
3. That black armband is hers.
4. Are these socks his?
5. These shirts are ours.
6. These gloves are hers.
7. Whose are these socks?
8. These boots are theirs.

UNIT 5
VOCABULARY
Exercise 1

a.

have	check	go
breakfast, a match, free time, training (also possible: social media)	social media, football scores	to the gym, to bed, home, shopping (also possible: training)

b. Your own answers

Exercise 2

a. 1. I check social media about a hundred times a day!
2. I usually go to bed before 11pm.
3. I go to the gym after work to keep fit!
4. My team usually have a match at 3pm on Saturdays.

b. Your own answers
c. Your own answers

VOCABULARY BUILDING
Exercise 1

relax, play games, listen to music: have free time
first half, half-time, second half: have a match
buy clothes, pay, discount: go shopping
share, like, follow: check social media

GRAMMAR
Exercise 1

1. has
2. has
3. have
4. eats
5. has
6. goes
7. has

Exercise 2

Your own answers

READING
Exercise 1

Two players talk about their kit: Jack (shirt) and Liam (underpants).

Exercise 2

Miguel: shower
Luca: check social media
Jack: start to walk down the tunnel
Harry: listen to heavy metal music
Liam: get changed into lucky underpants

Exercise 3

a. Your own answers
b. Your own answers

UNITS 1–5 REVIEW
VOCABULARY
Exercise 1

a. Player positions: forward, defender, central midfielder
Football verbs: pass, shoot, tackle
Set pieces: free kick, corner, kick-off
Places on the pitch: penalty box, halfway line, touchline
Football kit: socks, shorts, gloves, shin pads

Answer Key

b. Your own answers

Exercise 2

1. have
2. go
3. have
4. go
5. go
6. go
7. have
8. check

VOCABULARY BUILDING CHALLENGE

Unit 1: Argentinian, Portuguese, Italian
Unit 2: header, shot
Unit 3: crossbar, post
Unit 4 sleeves, badge, collar
Unit 5 Example answers: 1. buy clothes, pay, discount; 2. first half, second half, half-time

GRAMMAR
Exercise 1

1. isn't
2. is
3. aren't
4. shoots
5. pass
6. cross
7. Do
8. takes
9. Does
10. Whose
11. yours
12. my
13. have
14. doesn't
15. go

Exercise 2

1. mine
2. Do
3. are
4. pass
5. have
6. scores
7. has
8. takes

UNIT 6
VOCABULARY
Exercise 1

Head: ears, hair, nose, eyes, mouth, (neck)
Body: back, arm, shoulder, chest, (neck)
Legs: knee, shin, calf, ankle, hamstring, thigh

Exercise 2

Your own answers

VOCABULARY BUILDING
Exercise 1

Bones: broken
Joints: sprained
Muscles: pulled

Exercise 2

1. Pulled
2. sprained (the notes say that it isn't broken)
3. broken

GRAMMAR
Exercise 1

a. 1. Can you score from a throw-in?
2. Can you score from a corner?
3. Can you score from a goal kick?
4. Can the referee end a match early?
5. Can a goalkeeper take penalties?

b. A. No, you can't
B. Yes, you can
C. Yes, you can
D. Yes, they can
E. Yes, they can

Exercise 2

a. Your own answers
b. Your own answers

READING
Exercise 1

a. 1. Marinha
2. She has hurt (pulled or torn) her hamstring.
3. No, she can't.
4. Locomotive must play the final minutes of the game with 10 players only – they have no substitutions left.

90

b. 1. False: Nobody was near her.
2. True: Marinha missed 20 games last year with a hamstring injury.
3. True: She is Brazil's best player.
4. True: Diego says, 'That's it. She's out of the World Cup.' (We sometimes say that players are 'out' with an injury.)
5. False: Marinha can't walk off the pitch.

c. Breaking news! Marinha <u>out</u> of <u>World Cup</u> with <u>hamstring</u> injury.

UNIT 7
VOCABULARY
Exercise 1

fast – <u>slow</u>
short – <u>tall</u>
big – <u>small</u>
strong – <u>weak</u>
overweight – <u>slim</u>

Exercise 2

1. overweight
2. weak
3. slow
4. strong
5. big

VOCABULARY BUILDING
Exercise 1

Drawn answers may be different.
Suggested answers:

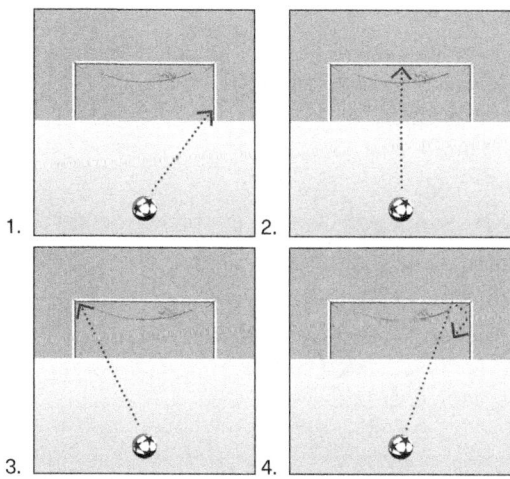

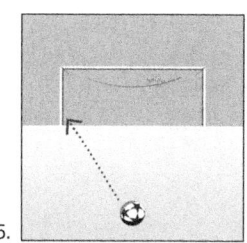

GRAMMAR
Exercise 1

a. 1. Haaland is a good finisher.
2. Donnarumma is a great goalkeeper.
3. De Ligt is a slow defender.
4. Mbappé is good in the air.
5. Macario is a skilful midfielder.
6. Ferran Torres is not / isn't good in the air.

b. Your own answers

Exercise 2

a. Your own answers
b. Your own answers

READING
Exercise 1

No: Locomotive need a strong defender, but Mann is weak in defence.

Exercise 2

+ :
Crossing: Mann has 4 assists from crosses this season.
Creating chances to score: Mann has 4 assists this season, and he assisted a goal in the game v Dynamo.
Passing: He had a 93% pass-completion rate against Dynamo.
Attacking: The scouts say he's a good attacking player.
Speed: He's very fast.
Two-footed: Mann plays on the right but is two-footed.

– :
Height: He's short.
Strength: He isn't strong. He doesn't defend well against more physical players.
Marking: He doesn't mark well from corners and free kicks.

Tackling: He doesn't win enough tackles.
Tackles won against Dynamo = only 70%.
Defending: He's weak in defence.
Heading: He isn't good in the air.

Exercise 3

Your own answer

UNIT 8
VOCABULARY
Exercise 1

Play it short
Push up
Drop off
Get tight
Hold the line
Switch it
Get goal-side
Clear it

Exercise 2

Suggested answers:
1. Get tight!
2. Push up!
3. Hold the line!
4. Time!
5. Man on!

VOCABULARY BUILDING
Exercise 1

1c; 2d; 3b; 4e; 5a

Exercise 2

1. Our ball!
2. Play him in!
3. What a ball!
4. Come on, ref!
5. Book him!

GRAMMAR
Exercise 1

1. don't
2. mark up
3. stand
4. Look
5. Get
6. get tight
7. Watch
8. Push up

READING
Exercise 1

Locomotive London 1 – 1 Manchester Athletic
Newcastle Town 3 – 1 Liverpool City

Exercise 2

a. 4
b. 5
c. 2
d. 1
e. 3

Exercise 3

Your own answers

UNIT 9
GRAMMAR
Exercise 1

1. was
2. were
3. was
4. was
5. was
6. was
7. had
8. scored
9. did not / didn't
10. scored
11. missed
12. saved

GRAMMAR BUILDING
Exercise 1

believe = believed
surprise = surprised
end = ended
lift = lifted
win = won

VOCABULARY
Exercise 1

1 syllable: played, passed, crossed, squared, pressed, fouled, marked, cleared
2 syllables: tackled, headed, lifted, dribbled
3 syllables: created

Exercise 2

1. tackled
2. dribbled
3. dribbled
4. kicked
5. missed
6. crossed
7. headed

Exercise 3

Your own answer

READING
Exercise 1

1c; 2b; 3d; 4a

Exercise 2

1. Senegal, France
2. Denmark, Germany
3. Brazil

Exercise 3

1. Germany (v Denmark), France (v Senegal)
2. Denmark (v Germany), Germany (v Brazil)
3. Brazil (the host nation)
4. Senegal (reached the quarter-finals, France out in the group stages), Denmark (beat World Cup holders, Germany, in Euro final)
5. France and Senegal

Exercise 4

Your own answers

UNIT 10
VOCABULARY
Exercise 1

1. three–one
2. two–two, two-all
3. zero–zero (this may be used in the USA), nil–nil (this is used in the UK)
4. six–nil

Exercise 2

1. beat
2. won
3. lost to
4. lost
5. beat
6. beat
7. won
8. lost to

Exercise 3

Your own answers

VOCABULARY BUILDING
Exercise 1

1d; 2b; 3e; 4f; 5g; 6c; 7a; 8h

Exercise 2

1. aggregate score
2. semi-final
3. delayed
4. home, away
5. knockout

GRAMMAR
Exercise 1

a.
1. Midlands Villa are playing away to Bristol FC.
2. South Coast are playing at home to Locomotive London.
3. Norfolk City are playing at home to Cardiff Central.
4. Liverpool City are playing away to Manchester Athletic.

b. W = Win; D = Draw

c. Suggested answers (your predictions may be different!):
I think Midlands Villa will beat Bristol FC.
I think South Coast will win against Locomotive London.
I think Cardiff Central will lose to Norfolk City.
I think Manchester Athletic v Liverpool will be a draw. (Note: You can use *a draw* as a noun.)

READING
Exercise 1

Adam <u>doesn't think</u> Harry will leave Locomotive.
Adam <u>doesn't think</u> Taka will join Manchester Athletic.

Answer Key

Exercise 2
1. Harry wants to play in the World Cup. (He needs regular first team football.)
2. He is only 21 years old; he can play in different positions.
3. They tried to sign him in the summer.
4. He's too expensive (Adam questions whether Athletic have enough money); it's too late in the transfer window for a big signing.

Exercise 3
Your own answers

UNITS 6–10 REVIEW
VOCABULARY
Exercise 1
Body parts: chest, hamstring, shoulder, thigh
Opposites: tall – *short*, strong – weak, fast – slow, big – small
Shouts: Mark up!, Easy ball!, Clear it!, Drop off!
Regular past simple verbs: crossed, dribbled, passed
Describing results: won, beat, drew

Exercise 2
1. beat
2. drew
3. won
4. lost to
5. drew
6. lost

GRAMMAR
Exercise 1
1. Can <u>you</u> score from a goal kick?
2. Can you be offside from <u>a</u> corner?
3. Konate is <u>a</u> strong defender.
4. Rapinoe <u>is</u> good on the ball.
5. Get <u>goal</u>-side!
6. Play <u>it</u> short!
7. She <u>missed</u> a penalty in the World Cup final.
8. He <u>didn't</u> shoot – he passed the ball to his teammate.
9. I think Manchester <u>will</u> win 2–1.
10. City are 10 points behind Athletic. They <u>won't</u> win the league.

Exercise 2
1. mark
2. cleared/clears
3. Was
4. headed/heads
5. saw
6. missed
7. lost
8. can't/cannot

VOCABULARY AND GRAMMAR BUILDING CHALLENGE
Unit 6: broken leg, pulled hamstring, sprained wrist
Unit 7: Example answers: in the bottom right/left corner, in the top right/left corner, in off the post, off the crossbar and in
Unit 8: Come on ref! Our ball!
Unit 9: believed, lifted, won
Unit 10: aggregate, semi-final

Notes

Notes

Notes

Also available from HATRIQA®

Football English Elementary Textbook

Learn to speak English like a Premier League Star

The Football English textbook helps students learn the English that's used in the professional game. Learn what to say on the pitch and off it and get yourself language-fit.

Available now at
www.hatriqa.com

Language Learner TRIQnotes

TRIQnotes are football-themed vocabulary notebooks for English. They are easy to use and work with the Football English Elementary Textbook to help you remember language more quickly.

Available now at
www.hatriqa.com

Jamie Johnson Graded Readers

"I almost feel like I am Jamie Johnson now!"
JUDE BELLINGHAM

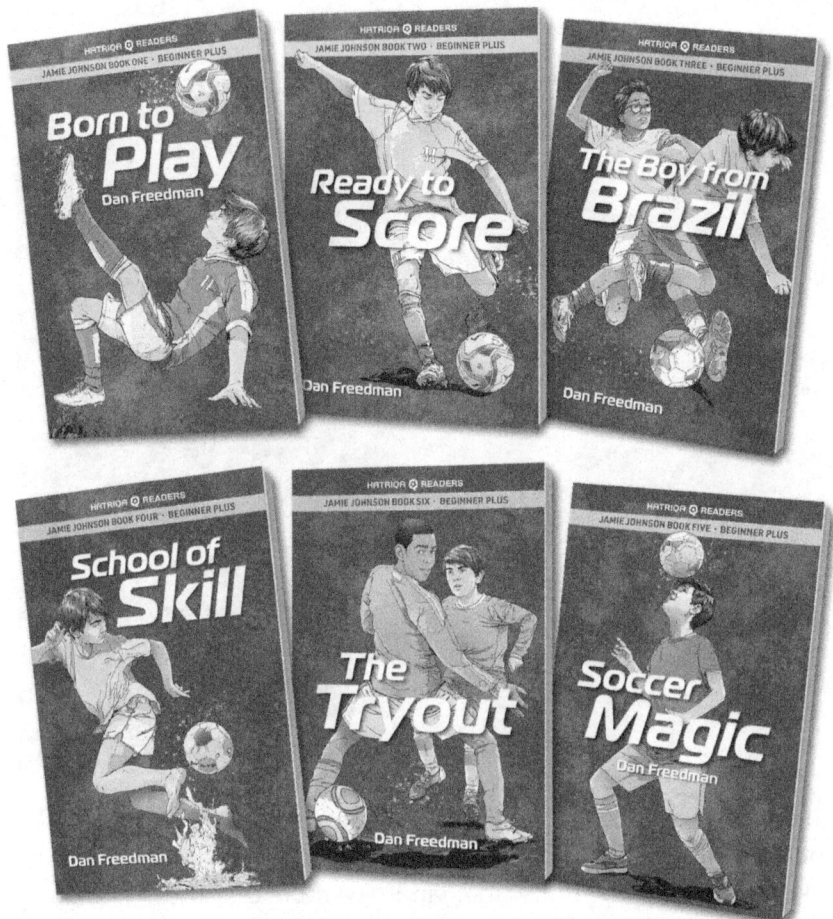

Based on the novels by Dan Freedman, the Jamie Johnson series tells the story of a boy who lives and breathes soccer. He has great skills, and he wants to get to the top. In each book in the series, we see Jamie as he learns more and follows his dream. He plans to become one of the greatest soccer players in the world.

HATRIQA's Soccer Reader® Series comprises the best in soccer fiction written as graded books for learners of English as a foreign language.

Available in paperback and ebook at
www.hatriqa.com

Printed in Dunstable, United Kingdom